"I have been encouraged greatly by the teachings of Chuck Smith over the years, and he has once again continued the encouragement by showing the beautiful depth of God's love for us, bathed in the promises of His Word. This book is an amazing example of loving the unlovable, and developing a deep understanding of God's heart for us, while continuing to stay grounded in God's Word."

Jeremy Camp
Best-selling Recording Artist
Dove Award Winner

"In a world where so many of us have caught "hurry sickness," Chuck Smith boldly reminds us that God's original plan for us is to be in a hurry to practice the art of love ... to perfect 'love as a lifestyle.' Be in a hurry to read this book and you will catch the urge to put love into action."

John Tesh
Author & Musician

"There are books, and then there are books. I would describe this new book from Chuck Smith—one of America's most influential pastors—as a lifework. *Love* was not written in some ivory tower of theory, and only a pastor like Chuck Smith could write about love so effectively.

"It was a love he and his wife, Kay, had in their hearts from the Lord to reach out to a lost generation of kids in the 1960s, which resulted in the *Jesus People Movement* in Southern California. I am proud to say that I was one of those kids who came to Christ through Chuck's ministry, and I now seek to reach this generation with that same life-changing message of the gospel. This is distilled truth that can potentially change your life. I highly recommend it."

Greg Laurie
Senior Pastor
Harvest Christian Fellowship, CA

“In the 1970s, when the world proclaimed a false and empty love—the love of God was poured out through the ministry of Pastor Chuck Smith. I was one of a generation transformed through his message.

“Pastor Chuck Smith writes with authority and great passion. No one can write a book on love unless they have truly encountered God personally. He is one of the most loving persons I have ever known. God has chosen His perfect writer! I know the message of this book is going to change people's hearts forever. There is a more excellent way—and it is the love of Christ!”

Raul Ries
Senior Pastor
Calvary Chapel Golden Springs, CA

“What could send a clearer signal that our faith in Christ is real than love? Chuck Smith highlights this greatest of all needs—to love and be loved—and shows how this is at the very heart of the gospel. In this book he demonstrates love's ‘trickle-down’ effect, how God's love for us transforms and prompts a response to love Him back, and then spills out to others in the most refreshing way. If you only read one book this year, let it be this one!”

Skip Heitzig
Senior Pastor
Calvary Chapel Albuquerque, NM

“Raised in the materialistic ‘50s, I soon fell for every lie the ‘60s had to offer. As hippies, we believed love was free, but I sacrificed my first-born son, my health, and many of my friends on that altar we called ‘free love.’ Chuck's new book is filled with strong biblical truths that are simple and easy to understand. This book will have a profound effect upon every reader who is a seeker of true love.”

Jeff Johnson
Senior Pastor
Calvary Chapel Downey, CA

"Reading this book brought me back to the early days of Calvary Chapel, where so many of our lives were forever changed by the simple, yet profound message of God's love.

"In the pages of *Love the More Excellent Way*, you will discover God's incredible, unbelievable, and merciful love for you. It changed a generation of kids back in the seventies, and this message of God's love can do it once again. Thank you, Pastor Chuck, for writing it out for us."

Steve Mays
Senior Pastor
Calvary Chapel South Bay, CA

"In a world that's so intent on questioning the God of the Bible—His existence, His character, His very nature—Pastor Chuck has clearly defined what the Bible teaches about the one true and living God, that at the heart of His very being, He is love! *Love, The More Excellent Way* not only reassures believers of God's everlasting love for them, but confronts us to re-evaluate how the 'love He has poured out in our hearts by the Holy Spirit' is demonstrated in our daily walk. In addition, non-believers are challenged to weigh the many Scriptures that declare His love for them, the world at large."

Richie Furay, Senior Pastor
Calvary Chapel Broomfield, CO
Buffalo Springfield Band Member

"Nearly forty years ago I walked into Calvary Chapel for the first time as a hippie. I was very skeptical, and not really open to Christianity. I was hoping that the minister might be a counter-culture person, but instead, my eyes were greeted by a normal 'straight-looking' person—Chuck Smith. His manner was soft and gentle, and his smile lit up the room.

"What I appreciated most about this book is what I have always appreciated from Chuck: his direct, simple, yet profound approach to teaching the Scriptures."

Chuck Girard
Christian Musical Artist
Love Song Band Member

"In a day and age when *love* is constantly redefined, Pastor Chuck takes us to the core definition: God is love. The immensity and power of God's love is overwhelming; being reminded of His unconditional love is humbling. The book has challenged me to love in ways beyond me … sacrificially."

Pancho Juarez
Senior Pastor
Calvary Chapel Montebello, CA

"The message of this book—authentic love—is vital to the salvation of our planet. When the world witnesses us experiencing and exhibiting the love of the Father, they will believe God is among us!"

Lee Ezell
Author & Speaker

"With all of the books I have read from Pastor Chuck—and I've read them all—this book touched me the most. I felt so close to Jesus reading it, and felt overwhelmed at times. I had to stop and wipe my eyes because of the tears.

"I know I will read it again—probably more than once. I felt like I was on the mountaintop, and I didn't want to come down. I will definitely get this for my friends and I am sure they will feel as blessed."

Christa Maletta
Customer Service for 22 Years
The Word For Today

LOVE

the more **EXCELLENT WAY**

Chuck Smith

THE WORD FOR TODAY

LOVE
by Chuck Smith

Published by The Word For Today
P.O. Box 8000, Costa Mesa, CA 92628

Web site: http://www.twft.com

(800) 272-WORD (9673)

ISBN: 9781597510417 (Paper)
ISBN: 9781597510400 (Cloth)

Printed in the United States of America.

Contents

INTRODUCTION: The More Excellent Way 9

PART ONE: God's Love for Us

1. Nothing Like It Anywhere 17
2. A Love Without Limits 33
3. A Love That Never Ends 53
4. Two Testaments, One Story 69
5. The Purpose of His Coming 87

PART TWO: Our Love for God

6. A New Heart 103
7. An Undivided Heart 117
8. A Heart That Loves Him Supremely 131
9. A Rekindled Heart 147
10. A Transformed Heart 161

PART THREE: God's Love Through Us to Others

11. Love Commanded 179
12. Love Described 193
13. Love in Action 207
14. Love Tested 221
15. Love as a Lifestyle 235

EPILOGUE: And Yet There Is More 249

INTRODUCTION
The More Excellent Way

FOR MANY YEARS I earnestly coveted the gifts of healing and the working of miracles. The book of Acts intrigued me with its many thrilling accounts of healing—especially since those healings accounted for an important facet of the apostles' ministry. So, I thoroughly studied the book. I read and reread every section of Scripture that dealt with healing.

As I witnessed the power of God manifested through the lives of the apostles, I came to desire that same power in my own life. I noted how God used those gifts of miracles and healing to draw thousands of people to the realization that Jesus rose from the dead and was alive and working in their hearts. And so I coveted those gifts. I prayed earnestly for them. I often drove out into the desert to fast and pray, asking the Lord to bestow upon me these potent gifts of His Spirit.

He didn't.

As the years rolled on, I began to understand His wisdom in refusing to grant me my request. It would be extremely difficult to have that kind of power working in your life unless you completely understood and continually practiced the Bible's message of death to self. When God begins to use a person in an obviously supernatural way, it generates a lot of attention—and observers tend to put such a person on a pedestal. As I looked back on my life, I realized that I could not have handled such notoriety or attention. And so I began to better appreciate the wisdom of God in not answering my prayers.

As decades came and went pastoring at different churches, I matured—something would be very wrong if I hadn't! And later being called to pastor at a church called Calvary Chapel Costa Mesa, I recognized that God had graciously blessed this church beyond measure. And I felt content.

Then one Monday night church service, the Spirit of God moved among us in a very special way. As I stood at the pulpit, I had a very strong consciousness of God's presence. I began to pray, thanking God for what He was doing and for the marvelous work of His Spirit in our church. I felt overwhelmed with God's goodness.

That night, close to a hundred young people came forward in response to an invitation to accept Christ as their Savior, and all of them went back to the prayer room. We sensed the beautiful moving of God's Spirit in our hearts. We all just stood together, worshiping the Lord and rejoicing over the wonderful work of His Spirit.

And then I brought up an old issue.

"Lord," I prayed silently, "I understand why in my early ministry You didn't give me the gifts of healings and the working of miracles. That was wise. I realize that I could not have handled it. But Lord, I think that maybe I have matured to the place where You could trust me with those now. We have such a marvelous moving of Your Spirit and the manifestation of Your gifts here in the church! How wonderful it would be if it was complete—if we saw all of the manifestations, including the working of miracles and the gifts of healing. I think, Lord, that perhaps You could trust me now. So I am open and willing."

Immediately the Lord spoke very clearly to my heart. "I have given to you the more excellent way," He said. "I have given you love."

"Thank You, Lord," I answered. "Subject closed."

Never again have I asked the Lord for those gifts. Instead, I will continue to walk in the way of love. I thank God for the privilege of walking in love.

A Profound Need for Love

A profound need to love and be loved lies at the very center of the human heart. Yet despite this obvious fact, the world clearly suffers from a shortage of love. In fact, our world screams for love.

Just look around. Everywhere you turn, you see the effects of people seeking love, desperately trying to fill their lives with *something*. When they cannot find true love, they turn to substitutes: drugs, sex, fame, fortune—anything to fill the hole in their soul.

"Chuck," you may say, "I disagree. I think there is plenty of love in the world. I love my kids, I love my spouse, I try to love my neighbor. I am full of love. And I know many other people who are just like me."

I understand. We are all in the process of trying to love—and in many cases, we really do show love to those around us. But the point is not, *do we love*? but rather, *do we love as God wants us to love*? In other words, do we love with the love of God in Christ? Sure, we love our family; yes, we love our friends; and at times, we might even love our neighbor. But many of us do not love as Jesus calls us to love—unconditionally, with grace, and influenced by the truth of God's Word.

That is the kind of love our world craves. And that is the only kind of love that will satisfy our deepest longings.

Our core problem, I believe, is that we badly misunderstand love. We think it has its source in us. It does not. To truly understand and practice love, we need to begin by grasping the true source: God Himself. *All* true love depends on God as its Author and Conduit. Otherwise, true love will never flow.

Genuine love begins with God and His unchanging character. God is love. In fact, He loved us long before we loved anything. The very act of our loving begins with God—in both receiving His love and returning that love. Only then can we fully love others.

This means that if you truly want to love a person, you must first understand God's love. Once you begin to grasp His love, you can begin to enthusiastically reflect it back to Him. And out of that delightful overflow, you can genuinely love others.

True love relies—*at every point*—upon God. Only then can love have its greatest effect in your life and in mine.

We All Need Love

Our church, Calvary Chapel of Costa Mesa, has sent out missionaries to assist orphanages in Romania. While we preach the gospel there and disciple the people, do you know what is one of our primary reasons for going? It's just to hold the infants. We want to cuddle them in our arms and love them.

Why?

Scientists tell us that an infant brain's development depends upon touch and love. Children, like all of us, desire to be loved upon. Too little attention of this kind can result in a condition known as "failure to thrive." If these infants do not get the love and touch they need, they become seriously at risk for lifelong mental and physical problems.

That's why we send out teams to love and hold the babies.

It intrigues me that even babies have an inborn desire to be loved. Just as interesting is that many adults have a desire to love those babies in return. People simply want to love and be loved.

Clearly, the Lord has implanted this need for love deep within us. As human beings created in God's image, we reflect Him who is love. The Bible describes love as a mutual exchange of giving and receiving—and we embrace this mutual exchange when we love God and love one another.

The wonderful reality of love is this: God so loved the world that He sent Jesus, His Son, to lay down His life on our behalf. And now He calls us, His people, to spend our days loving as Jesus would have us love, through the power of the Holy Spirit. That's what this book is all about.

First, I want to encourage us to gaze for a little while into the loving eyes of our heavenly Father. Secondly, I want to motivate us to reflect that divine love back to the Source. And thirdly, I want to challenge us to direct His love to the people around us—to those whom Jesus died to save.

Love is a magnificent and glorious truth of who God is. The Lord is our great example of love. And we fulfill His purpose for us when we become conduits of His love to those who desperately need it.

PART ONE

God's Love for Us

"And we have known and believed the love that God has for us."

1 JOHN 4:16

If you ever want to approach God for anything, it is vitally important that you understand His character. If you do not know that God is merciful, then it will be difficult for you to ask Him for mercy. If you do not realize that He is gracious, then it will be difficult for you to ask Him for grace. Knowing the character of God gives you the rock-solid confidence to come to Him with joyful expectancy.

And here's the great Bible truth about God's character: *He is love* (1 John 4:8, 16). God's love never fails! God has never stopped loving you. He does not love you when you are good and hate you when you are bad. God's love for you remains constant and unchanging. It cannot fail. God continually pours out His love upon your life, for His love for you does not depend upon what you are, but upon Who *He* is.

And quite simply, "God is love." That's the place to begin.

Nothing Like It Anywhere

THE MASSIVE CULTURE SHIFTS of the 1960s ushered in tumultuous times. What we had always known as America, informed by a Christian worldview, began to morph before our eyes into something very different. As my wife, Kay, and I watched the protest signs held up by the youth of the day—*Peace! Love! Understanding!*—our hearts broke. Not because these young people wanted peace, love, or understanding, but that they sought them in all the wrong places: in free love, political radicalism, drugs, and Eastern mysticism. We knew that such a search—regardless of how earnest—could never bring them the peace, love, or understanding they craved.

I can still remember the day the hippies began invading our neighborhood. As I looked at these kids in their old vans, long hair, granny glasses, bare feet and dirty jeans, I thought, *You dirty hippies! Why don't you get a job and live right? Cut your hair and go to work!*

Kay had a very different reaction. She cried. And then she said, "Oh, those poor children! They need to know Jesus."

God apparently agreed with her, because before long I heard the Lord saying to me, "I have many people who happen to be hippies; they are Mine. All they need to know is My love and the peace that I can give them." But as I looked at these young people from a purely human perspective, I thought, *That's the most unlikely group* ***ever*** *to try to evangelize.*

To my amazement, however, we saw the Lord reach into that subculture and begin to draw to Himself thousands of eager young disciples. God saw into the hearts of those young men and women and knew that many of them were just searching after truth, searching after love, and searching after peace.

As Kay continued to watch the hippies move into our corner of Southern California, her heart softened more and more. Then, one day, she saw a hippie girl in a flowing dress staggering down the street. The young woman looked totally lost as she stared into a storefront window. At that moment, the Lord made it clear to Kay that our family was to begin a love story of sorts—a story of watching the love of God penetrate the lives of untold numbers of young seekers in what became known as the "Jesus People Movement." From then on we began to share the love of God with these hippies, reaching out to them with the love of Christ.

Our hearts rejoiced as we saw thousands of young men and women find real peace, love, and understanding through a saving knowledge of Jesus Christ. It thrilled us to watch the Lord use these young people to reach out with love to their contemporaries as they represented the Lord with joy, enthusiasm, and charity. It may have been the "summer of love" for some, but for many others, it became an era of true love … discovering God's love for them.

In fact, this is exactly where the journey must begin for all of us.

We must all come to know and experience—for ourselves—God's amazing love.

The Stunning Power of Love

What an incredibly potent force love is! While it lacks the clout that some attribute to it—science will never agree that "*Love makes the world go around,*" as one old song insists—yet, I know for certain that it keeps *me* going in the world that does go around.

Love is the force that prompts you to go the extra mile. Love makes your life worthwhile. Love makes you get up and try again. History overflows with stories of men and women whose love motivated them to heroic acts. Others have endured extreme hardship because of love. The power of love still prompts others to rise against imposing challenges, throwing back what appear to be insurmountable odds.

What a powerful force is love! Nothing stronger or deeper exists.

A mother's love is legendary. In fact, should a mother desert her offspring, we mentally put her on a level with the animals. Scripture itself describes such a mother as "without natural affection" (Romans 1:31; 2 Timothy 3:3). We all expect a strong, natural bond to unite a loving mother with the child of her womb. I thank God for the privilege of experiencing this natural bond. My mother showered her love upon us in so many special ways.

And again years later, I saw the same kind of motherly love as I watched my wife continually demonstrate her undying commitment to our children. I saw how love motivated Kay to spend long, agonizing hours in prayer during those difficult times when our children struggled mightily, when their destinies hung in the balance. And yet, what a beautiful thing to see my determined wife's constant intercession, her refusal to let go, her holding on in prayer—all motivated by love. The strong bond of a mother's love makes incredible sacrifices.

Then I think of the love of a man for his bride. As a pastor, I get a bird's eye view of this kind of love as I stand before a young couple on their wedding day. I watch them as they lovingly gaze into each other's eyes, peering deeply into the other's soul. I'm close enough that I can read the quivering lips that silently mouth, "I love you." I observe their bodies almost tremble with excitement when that special moment arrives, calling for them to declare their covenant of love by saying out loud, "Until death do us part." And so they commit their lives to one another—for better, for worse, for richer, for poorer, in sickness and in health. A covenant of love brings them to the altar.

We see an even greater covenant of love in the elderly couple that has celebrated fifty or more years together. They have weathered all the storms. They've made it through the hurricanes and the blizzards and the droughts. Now they enjoy a bond so deep and so strong that to communicate effectively they don't even have to speak to each other. They know what the other is thinking and they can accurately predict the words before their mate utters them. To see them holding hands, to watch them gazing at each other through years of rich experience—it nearly makes me weep. How beautiful is such an enduring covenant of love.

And then there is the love of camaraderie, a fraternal kind of love, a deep love that some fortunate men experience in their closest friendships. As they work with each other or fight alongside one another or play on a team together, their mutual admiration grows strong through times of extreme challenge and even danger. This is the kind of love that causes a man to throw his body down on a live grenade in order to save the lives of the men in his platoon. Best-selling books are written on the basis of such tremendous acts of heroism motivated by love. As Jesus said, "Greater love has no one than this, than to lay down one's life for his friends" (John 15:13).

But the covenant of love I want to highlight here is far greater than that of a mother for her child, a husband for his wife, or a soldier for his comrades-in-arms. The greatest covenant of love in the universe is the one that God seeks to make with you today.

A Gift Beyond Comprehension

God loves you with a love that defies human understanding. The apostle Paul prayed that the Christian believers of ancient Ephesus might know the love of Christ, which, he said, far exceeds human understanding:

> That you may be able to comprehend with all the saints what is the breadth, and the length, and the depth, and the height; and to know the love of Christ, which passes knowledge (Ephesians 3:18-19).

Frankly, this request fascinates me. How can you "know" something that far surpasses your ability to comprehend it? Paul gives us a clue through the word translated "know" (*ginosko*), which in the original language means, "to know by experience." You can "know" this love only by experiencing it for yourself. You cannot "know" it by having someone tell you about it. You have to experience it for yourself to fully appreciate the depth of God's love for you.

So the apostle prays something like this: "God loves you so much, I pray that you might know the depth of God's love for you, the length of God's love, the height of God's love. If you could only fathom the depth to which Jesus was willing to come in order to redeem you! If you could only explore the height to which God intends to bring you, that He might seat you together with Christ in heavenly places and make you a joint heir with Him in His eternal kingdom! If only you could see the length to which God is willing to go to save you."

The broadness of God's love encompasses all of humankind, every race, tribe, and nation. It reaches to all men and women, boys and girls. No one lies outside of the boundaries of God's love. Best of all, His love for you—its breadth, its length, its height, its depth—will last forever.

That is why some fifty times in the Bible we read, "His mercy [or love] endures forever."

God most clearly manifested the depth of His love for you on the cross. Jesus, who eternally existed in the form of God, emptied Himself and came to earth in the likeness of man. As a servant, He remained obedient unto death, even the death of the cross. That's how deep the love of God is for you. Jesus willingly died in your place.

When God sent Jesus to earth, He gave us His very best. That's the crowning characteristic of love—it wants to give its best. Suppose I found a bouquet of wilted flowers in a dumpster, pulled them out of the trash, arranged them haphazardly, and finally took them home to my wife. Would you be impressed? Probably not—and neither would Kay. Nor would it help my cause much to say, "I love you, dear. See? Here are some wilted flowers."

While I've never given Kay flowers extracted from a dumpster, many times after a funeral I have had the opportunity to take her some gorgeous bouquets. People leave them at the church and say, "Do with them what you want." A few times I have brought home some hundred-dollar bouquets, filled with orchids and other gorgeous and even exotic flowers. And do you know what she says to me?

"Did you have a funeral today?"

Because I got them for free—though they cost someone a bundle—the gesture didn't mean much to her. It certainly didn't mean as much to her as if I had stopped to pick up a small bunch of carnations at a little corner stand run by some enterprising kids.

True love wants to show itself through extravagant giving—and God sought to show you the magnitude of His love by giving you His best. It cost God *tremendously* to show you the depth of His love. In fact, we will never be able to comprehend how much He gave when He sent us His only begotten Son, Jesus. Such an extravagant gift proves how much He cares for you.

A Gift We Didn't Deserve

When I bring home flowers to Kay, I do so because she's worth it. She deserves far more than flowers, of course, but pretty bouquets represent my love for this woman who deserves my very best. God's gift of His Son far surpasses anything like that. In fact, He gave us His best when we deserved His worst:

> But God demonstrated [or manifested] His love toward us in that while we were yet sinners, Christ died for us (Romans 5:8).

Jesus died for the ungodly, not for the worthy. He died for us when we were yet sinners, not when we were saints. He willingly went to the cross while we were still in open rebellion against Him, still coming short of His glory, still missing the mark—and yet God manifested His love for us by having Christ die for us *even then.*

We *weren't* righteous. We *weren't* good. We *weren't* lovely. But God showed the vastness of His love for us by sending His only begotten Son to die on our behalf, *while we were still sinners.*

When did God start loving you? Was it when you surrendered your life to Jesus Christ? When you raised your hand and went forward at some church service or evangelistic event? When you said the sinner's prayer? Did God say at that moment, "Oh, isn't that sweet? I am going to love him now"? No! God displayed His love toward you in that while you were yet a sinner, Christ died for you—ungodly you.

Because Jesus died for sinners, we have nothing to boast about in and of ourselves. "Well, the Lord died for me because He saw I was doing my best. He knew I was trying hard. He knew I had potential." No! Christ died for you and me when we were still sinners, even as we wallowed in our ungodly filth. God loved us even then.

So often we imagine that God must feel disgusted with us, disappointed, discouraged, or even through with us. We feel sure He must have a terribly negative attitude toward us.

Years ago, my daughter Jan started going through that "nobody-loves-me" routine after receiving a reprimand. She declared that none of her friends loved her, that her mother and daddy didn't love her, that *nobody* loved her.

"Oh, yes, we love you," we told our little girl.

"No, you don't," she insisted.

When she displayed no signs of giving in, I finally said, "Well, Jesus loves you."

"Oh, no, He doesn't," she immediately replied.

"What?" I asked, a little stunned.

"He *doesn't,*" she repeated. "He just popped His head out of the clouds and stuck His tongue out at me!"

Sometimes we imagine Jesus doing that to us; don't we? We tell ourselves that He's had it with us—that He's "out of here." Now, while I could understand Him doing such a thing, He never will. He knew what He got when He died for us. Remember the truth: "God commended His love toward us in that while we were yet sinners, Christ died for us" (Romans 5:8).

An Eternal Covenant of Love

The apostle John tells us,

> Herein is love, not that we loved God, but that God loved us and sent His Son to be the propitiation for our sins (1 John 4:10).

God loved you from eternity past and now seeks to enter a covenant of love with you. God's love for you is so great that He wants to spend eternity with you—not, "until death do us part," but "until death unites us forever."

On the night before His crucifixion, Jesus took a cup of wine and said to His disciples, "This cup is the new covenant in My blood, which is shed for you" (Luke 22:20). This new covenant is a love covenant. Because of God's great love, Jesus gave His life for you. He took your sins, your guilt, your condemnation, your just desserts. He took the penalty and the wrath of God against you and your sin, and in its place He established God's love covenant with you through His death.

And now God invites you to enter into that love covenant with Him. He wants you to become His child so that He can live His life through you. He wants others to know of His love through you.

Many parents, dads especially, like to live their lives through their sons. My dad was no exception. When I was just two years old, he put a glove in my hand and started throwing baseballs to me. By the time I was four, I could proficiently field any ball. Dad always seemed to be throwing footballs at me, or putting a basketball hoop in the yard, or driving me to a tennis court. In my teen years after I scored a touchdown, I could always hear my dad's voice above the thousands of fans yelling and cheering. He could out-yell them all! I'm told that he would bow to the people in the stands and say, "That's my son."

In a sense, my dad lived his life through his son, hoping that my achievements would exceed his. I knew he felt proud of me, his son, and gloried in the acclaim that came to me through my athletic exploits.

I think our heavenly Father feels much the same. At two special moments in the earthly life of Jesus, God took great pains to say, "That's My boy!" At Jesus' baptism, for example, a voice rang out from heaven:

"This is My beloved Son, in whom I am well pleased" (Matthew 3:17). In other words, "Hey, folks—that's My boy!" Again at the Mount of Transfiguration, God said, "This is My beloved Son, in whom I am well pleased. Hear Him!" (Matthew 17:5).

Today, your Father God wants to live His life through you. As you enter into this covenant of love, it becomes possible for God to express His life—His nature, His desires, and His actions—through you. God wants your life to testify to Who He is. He wants you to do great exploits for Him. By entering into this love covenant with God, the Lord can begin to use you to reveal Himself to the world around you.

Through this love covenant, God agrees to provide for you and to take care of you. He pledges to watch over you, to keep you, to shield you and to protect you. The author of Psalm 91 begins by writing,

> He who dwells in the secret place of the Most High shall abide under the shadow of the Almighty. I will say of the Lord, "He is my refuge and my fortress; My God, in Him I will trust" (Psalm 91:1-2).

By the end of the psalm, God Himself starts speaking:

> Because he has set his love upon Me, therefore I will deliver him; I will set him on high, because he has known My name. He shall call upon Me, and I will answer him; I will be with him in trouble; I will deliver him and honor him. With long life I will satisfy him, and show him My salvation (vv. 14-16).

That's God describing what He'll do for *you* when you enter into this love covenant with Him. All of these rich blessings and amazing benefits are yours when you "set your love upon Him."

And ultimately, God will bring you into His very presence in heaven, that you might dwell with Him forever. Throughout the ages to come, He will reveal to you the exceeding richness of His love and kindness toward you in Christ Jesus. God loves you so much that it's going to take all of eternity to reveal it. As the old hymn rightly says,

> Could we with ink the ocean fill, and were the skies of parchment made, were every blade of grass a quill, and every man a scribe by trade, to write the love of God above, would drain the oceans dry. Nor could the scroll contain the whole, though stretched from sky to sky. O love of God, how rich and pure! How measureless and strong![1]

God loves me. God loves you. And He wants to enter into a love covenant with you today.

His Banner Over You

Several years ago we received an invitation to join the king of Tonga for a celebration of his birthday. We gathered with hundreds of others on a soccer field where we saw table after table—some 300 feet long—loaded with food. There had to be a quarter of a mile of savory dishes covering these tables—succulent pigs and all kinds of fruit, and too many culinary delights to number.

Each island group invited to the feast had a banner above its assigned table so that the guests could know where to sit. Soon we found our group and we sat down to enjoy a thoroughly memorable meal. I've never seen so much food! The king provided a fabulous royal banquet to celebrate his birthday. And as I sat there, I couldn't help but think of a favorite Scripture from the Old Testament:

> He brought me to the banqueting house, and his banner over me was love (Song of Solomon 2:4).

Have you ever entered a large banquet hall where a grand dinner was about to be served? Perhaps you saw thousands of settings but didn't know where you were to sit. So you started searching to find the right place, but nothing looked promising. Finally you spotted a familiar banner across the hall and you made your way over to it. There you began looking on the table for your own nametag. When at last you found your place, you said, "There is my nametag. Here is where I sit." And so you sat down and waited for the meal to begin.

---

1 *The Love of God*, written by Frederick M. Lehman, 1919.

Jesus has given you just such a special place. Can you see it? His banner over you is love. He loves you more than you can understand, more than you can know. His love for you is far better than unconditional. He loves you actively, personally, thoughtfully. And He does so knowing everything about you.

During courtship we often do our best to hide the truth about ourselves. We have come to love this person and we fear that if he or she knew the whole truth, the love would end. And so we go in with a bit of deceit.

Maybe he spills a soda on you and you say, "Oh, that's all right. My, that doesn't matter a bit. I can get it cleaned, no problem." While inside you're thinking, *You clumsy oaf! What's wrong with you?* Or maybe he takes you out to McDonald's for three nights in a row. You smile and say, "McDonald's, how wonderful. I think that's great! Yes, I like fries and Big Macs." And you act so sweet. But beneath the smiles you're thinking, *You cheapskate, why don't you take me someplace where they use plates?*

We don't dare reveal the truth, however, because we want this person to think we're always sweet and smiling. We never get angry or upset. We always present ourselves as the very soul of graciousness.

Now, why do we engage in such deceit? We do so because we're afraid that if this person knew the real truth, he or she might stop liking us. So we keep it up until the day we get married—and then what a shock we get as our beloved begins to express his or her real feelings and we learn the truth.

Frankly, this is the wonderful thing about the love of Jesus. *He knew the truth about you all the while!* Before you ever enter His covenant of love, He already knows all there is to know about you—even things you don't know yourself. He knows every one of your bad qualities—and loves you anyhow. He loves you despite your weaknesses. The Lord knows you backwards and forwards, inside and out, upside and down, and yet still He loves you. So He invites you to His banqueting table and His banner over you is love. He wishes to announce to the whole assembly, to the world, "This is the one I love. This is My beloved."

Love, Not Law

The Lord doesn't want a merely legal relationship with you. He doesn't want you to obey Him only because you fear the consequences of disobedience. I think we often make a big mistake when we try to emphasize the judgment of God upon the disobedient. We try to dangle men and women over the pit of hell and put the fear of God in their hearts. So they sit there, quivering and shaking in the presence of God, afraid to smile or do anything else lest they get snuffed. Soon they develop a relationship with God that scares them silly; they obey only because they don't want to get fried. And so they get stuck in a legal relationship with God.

But the Lord doesn't want that kind of a relationship with you, any more than you want that kind of a relationship with your wife or husband: "You'd better do it, baby, or I'll beat the tar out of you." I want my wife to partner with me because she loves me, not because she fears my terrible temper.

Paul said the love of Christ "compelled" him (2 Corinthians 5:14). The love of Jesus motivated the apostle to risk his life for the gospel. It was His love that drew him. So he could also say of Jesus, "He invites me into His banqueting house and His banner over me is love."

The love of God goes beyond anything we know on the human plane. You've never experienced such a love. It's a constant love, a pure love, a strong love, a love that overcomes your weaknesses and failures, and seeks only your good and your best. Many times you'll discover God's love the most when you have been at your worst. It is then that you realize how much He loves you.

Oftentimes after I've had a bad day and been out of sorts and am down on myself, God will do something special for me—just some neat, little thing with big, bold letters all over it: "I love you." And I say, "Lord, I can't believe this. You're so good!" When I feel miserable and unworthy and undeserving, that's exactly when God seeks to show me His love. His love for me doesn't alter from day to day with my mood shifts or my temperament. His love is constant and enduring. He loves me with an everlasting love, with a love that doesn't stop or diminish.

And He loves you in exactly the same way.

Taste and See

God loves you! And He invites you to experience for yourself how good His love truly is.

"Oh, taste and see that the Lord is good," the Bible says (Psalm 34:8). You cannot really know God's love until you taste it for yourself. Certainly, I can tell you about it. I can describe how good it feels to walk with the Lord. I can write about my wonderful experience of His love. I can list some of the great things the Lord does for me and wants to do for you—but you will never really *know* until you taste it for yourself.

You may say, "Well, I'm glad it has helped you, but it's not for me." A lot of people have that attitude; they just won't taste for themselves. Or they'll say, "It's good that you found something that satisfies you. That's nice. I'm happy that you're not on drugs anymore. I'm glad for you." But they refuse to taste for themselves. God says, "Oh, taste and see that the Lord is good."

Life in Christ is so rich that it can be described only in superlatives. Jesus said, "I have come that they may have life," but then He quickly added, "and that they may have it more abundantly" (John 10:10). Jesus offers not just life, but full, rich, abundant life. In the same way, when Peter testifies to the joy we have in Jesus, he does not simply say, "We have great joy in the Lord." Instead he writes of a "joy inexpressible and full of glory" (1 Peter 1:8). You cannot describe that joy; it's too full of glory. Likewise, when the Scripture speaks about the peace available to us in Christ, it doesn't only say, "You'll have real peace in Jesus." No, it describes a peace from God that surpasses all human understanding (Philippians 4:7).

You have never experienced anything that can equal the love of Christ. His love exceeds anything that you can know or feel on a human level. There is no vocabulary, no words that can adequately describe the stupendous things God has for those who love Him, who are drawn by His love to Himself. But to know that, you have to *taste*: "Oh, taste and see that the Lord is good."

Have you tasted? Once you do, then you'll be able to say along with the delighted bride of Solomon, "His fruit was sweet to my taste" (Song of Solomon 2:3).

A Love Without Limits

JUST HOW BIG IS God's love? How much ground does His love cover? Psalm 103:11 helps answer the question when it declares, "For as the heavens are high above the earth, so great is His mercy [or love] toward those who fear Him."

So how high are the heavens above the earth? Astronomy has advanced rapidly in the past few years, especially with the advent of new telescopes and new ways of probing deeper into the observable universe. Equipped with this knowledge, can scientists tell us how high the heavens are above the earth? Until recently, astronomers put the distance at twelve billion light years—that was the farthest they could peer into the cosmos. But now, using better telescopes, they have seen new galaxies some fifteen billion light years away.

God's mercy and love just grew by three billion light years!

I imagine they'll find out the universe is more vast than that. How exciting! The more astronomers discover, the more I will see of God's love toward me—ever higher and ever greater. So keep searching, fellows. You're only expanding the love of my God. When I feel, *Man, I must have reached His limit,* then they discover more galaxies another two or three—or five billion light years more distant. "*All right!*" I say with a breath of relief. "God's love will cover me for a long time."

It Gets Better

No astronomer will ever be able to limit the love of God, for the psalmist writes, "As far as the east is from the west, so far has He removed our transgressions from us" (Psalm 103:12). Just imagine what it would mean had the author used the phrase, "as far as the north is from the south," rather than what he actually did write, "as far as the east is from the west." The north lies only about 12,500 miles from the south. You can travel north only until you get to the North Pole; then you begin heading south again. And as soon as you reach the South Pole, then you start going north once more. To have your sins removed 12,500 miles from you would be good—but not *nearly* as good as what God's love has provided for you.

If you started flying east tonight, you would continue to fly east for the rest of your life, so long as you didn't change directions or run out of fuel. Or if you started flying due west, you'd keep flying west for all of eternity.

Oh, how glad I am that God inspired the writer to say, "as far as the east is from the west," rather than, "as far as the north is from the south!" I want my sins taken away from me farther than the north lies from the south. I like the idea of God *completely* removing my sins and my guilt—and all because of His infinite love and mercy.

Love Defined

One morning I listened to a news commentator describe how we are constantly adding words to our dictionary. The analyst suggested that whenever we add a new word, the speakers who make the word popular—especially newscasters—at first use the term to convey a very specific and definite meaning. But after a short while, listeners who adopt the new term tend to make it go in a hundred other directions.

The question for us here is this: What does God mean by the term "love"?

Unfortunately, English doesn't do an adequate job of conveying everything God wants to express through the term. I can say, for example, "I love my wife, Kay," to express my deepest feelings and emotions for her. Yet when I want to describe what I think about hot fudge sundaes, English makes me use the same word: "I *love* hot fudge sundaes!" Let me assure you, however, that even though I use the same word "love," what I feel toward hot fudge sundaes differs profoundly from what I feel toward my wife! We use our single English word "love" to describe a wide spectrum of emotions and states of being.

Ancient Greek, on the other hand—the language of the New Testament—used three main words to express the idea of love. The Greeks understood that man existed on three levels: the physical, the emotional, and the spiritual. While the Greeks didn't understand very well the spiritual level, they did grasp the physical and the emotional.

They used the word *eros* to describe love on a physical level. In Greek mythology, Eros was the god of love and the consort of Aphrodite, the Greek goddess of passion and physical love. Today, when Hollywood talks about love, usually it's talking about the Greek idea of *eros*. It focuses on the physical level of love, the erotic—which isn't always love. Such love tends to be extremely self-centered and constantly seeks self-gratification. Most often it could better be translated "lust." So when a person on the silver screen purrs, "Let's make love," it isn't necessarily love at all. It's interesting to note that the New Testament doesn't use the term *eros* even once.

The ancient Greeks usually employed the words, *phileo* or *storge*, to describe fondness or friendship. This is the natural affection a man has for his children, the love a mother has for her family, or the love you have for your friends. This is love on the emotional level, the kind of love one has for grandchildren and great grandchildren. It's the kind of love you experience in good relationships with others. It describes a deep kinship and bond that ties human lives together. The name "Philadelphia" combines two Greek words: *phileo* ("love") and *adelphos* ("brotherly"); therefore, Philadelphia is the "city of brotherly love." When God tells wives to "love" their husbands, He uses the term *phileo*. Or when He tells older women to teach younger women to "love" their husbands, again He uses the term *phileo*—fondness, respect, love.

Phileo or *storge* is usually reciprocal. "I love you because you love me. I love you because we get along well. We are able to relate to each other and understand each other. We like the same kind of music. We like the same kind of books. Since we have these affinities and seem to complement each other, therefore I have this fondness for you in the *phileo* realm." It's a reciprocal kind of love, a genuine give-and-take. The New Testament uses this term some twenty-two times.

But when you enter the realm of the Spirit—which neither the ancient Greeks nor the modern secular world knows—you find a depth of love that transcends basic human love. *Agape* speaks of a dimension of love far greater than emotions and much deeper than just physical attraction. It's a spiritual love that comes from the deepest part of a person's being. This love does not look for something in return. It does not seek reciprocity, but simply reaches out to embrace the object of its love.

Since such a divine concept did not exist at the time the New Testament took shape, its writers took a little-used Greek word and transformed it to express a depth of love that transcends physical love or emotional love—a self-sacrificing love. And thus, the New Testament writers essentially coined the word *agape* to describe a giving, selfless kind of love.

It is this word that the New Testament consistently uses to describe God's loving, expansive attitude toward us. Think of it! His love for us is so deep, so great that the writers of the New Testament basically had to invent a word to portray the vastness of its depth, strength, and power.

Rich in Mercy, Great in Love

How big is God's love? We get the best answer of all when we look at the cross of Jesus Christ.

We were all hopelessly lost, bound by Satan's power and a slave to the devil and to our own unredeemed flesh—but God intervened because of His great love for us. He wasn't willing that we should perish and go down the tubes. As the apostle Paul wrote,

> But God, who is rich in mercy, because of His great love with which He loved us, even when we were dead in trespasses, made us alive together with Christ (Ephesians 2:4-5).

There it is! God is "rich" in mercy and "great" in love. Even when we lived for our sin and flaunted our trespasses—even while we remained totally alienated from God—yet God loved us.

Why? *Because God is love*. That is the essence and nature of God's being. That's what He's all about. As the original Greek would say it, *theos agape esten*, "God love is" (1 John 4:8). And how did God show the magnitude of His love for us? The apostle John would answer,

> In this the love of God was manifested toward us, that God has sent His only begotten Son into the world, that we might live through Him (1 John 4:9).

There is the manifestation. *There* is the proof. How did God most powerfully demonstrate the magnitude of His love? By sending His Son into the world that we might live through Him. Every Good Friday when we gather to remember the death of Jesus Christ—His suffering, His pain, His agony—we should remember it for what it is, an amazing demonstration of God's love.

I find it interesting that the Bible never seeks to prove God's love to us apart from the cross. Whenever the Bible wants to exhibit the fact of God's love, it always points to Calvary. "God demonstrates His own love toward us," Paul wrote, "in that while we were still sinners, Christ died for us" (Romans 5:8).

We don't learn much about God's love from nature. It can bring us to the awareness of God's existence, but not much more. That is why every culture in the world has some consciousness of the existence of God. Nature gives us a very powerful witness to His reality.

But the only nature we see on earth is fallen, corrupted by our sin. Consider the marvelous design of the gazelle; it has elegant grace and exceptional speed. That gazelle testifies to a marvelous divine design. But watch it long enough, and you might see a lion wrestle that gazelle to the ground and devour it. Nature alone cannot tell you that God is love. Only in the Bible do we get the clear revelation that God is love.

Neither does man-made religion teach us that God is love. Greek mythology, for example, tells us that god is lust. Many religions promote hatred. Hate pours out when their adherents say, "If you don't believe, we'll kill you." Only in the Bible do we get the consistent revelation that God is love—and the greatest proof it offers is the cross. *There* God manifested the full extent of His love for us.

> In this is love, not that we loved God, but that He loved us and sent His Son [to be] the propitiation for our sins (1 John 4:10).

It is through Jesus that we are made spiritually alive. We are born again by the Spirit of God; our spirit comes alive, and as it does, we begin to know God and His amazing love.

John writes,

> And he is the propitiation for our sins: and not for ours only, but also for [the sins of] the whole world. (1 John 2:2).

How many people have you heard say, "I love God"? Now, that's no big deal. Many people *say* they love God—but what they feel is not necessarily love. True love is God sending His Son to rescue us from our sins. Now that's a *big* deal! God loves us despite all our imperfections and failures.

This word "propitiation" has an interesting history. In Hebrew it appears as the term *kophar*, which means "a covering." The Old Testament uses the word to describe the mercy seat, the lid on the ark of the covenant. On that lid stood two golden cherubim facing each other. The whole ark was designed to model what exists in heaven: God seated upon the mercy seat, surrounded by angelic creatures called cherubim.

Inside the ark of the covenant lay the two tablets of stone upon which God had engraved the Ten Commandments. Interesting how the mercy seat hovered over the law. Once a year, the high priest came into the Holy of Holies before the ark of the covenant to sprinkle the blood of the sacrifice on the mercy seat. This signified a covering for their sins, as the priest sprinkled blood on the mercy seat situated over the law—very symbolic and very powerful.

John tells us that Jesus, on the cross, became that *covering* for our sins. He took our sins upon Himself and satisfied God's justice by bearing our sins in His own body on the cross (see also 1 Peter 2:24). *That* is love! *That* is grace! And that is what God willingly did for you and for me, thus demonstrating His mammoth love.

In the book of Hosea God says of His people, "I will heal their backsliding, I will love them freely" (14:4). I love that! God loves us *freely*. Centuries after Hosea's time, Paul echoed his predecessor when he wrote,

> He who did not spare His own Son, but delivered Him up for us all, how shall He not with Him also freely give us all things? (Romans 8:32).

So here's the question: If God has freely given you and me that much already, then how much more will He willingly give us the little things we need from day to day?

What Manner of Love

The love of God is so great and so rich that He willingly sacrificed His only begotten Son, Jesus Christ, to enable you to become a son or a daughter of God by believing in Him. Through faith in Jesus, you are adopted into the family of God and made an heir of God, and a joint heir with Jesus Christ.

Can any of us fully comprehend this truth? I doubt it. Probably the best we can do is to stand in awe of it, as did the apostles.

Just how huge is the love of God? How great is it? "Greater love," Jesus said, "has no one than this, than to lay down one's life for his friends" (John 15:13). As John marveled over the willing self-sacrifice of Jesus, he couldn't help but write, "Behold what manner of love the Father has bestowed upon us, that we should be called children of God!" (1 John 3:1).

Centuries before the Savior finally arrived on planet Earth, the psalmist wrote, "Let Your mercy, O Lord, be upon us, just as we hope in You" (Psalm 33:22). As you hope in God, He will show you His extraordinary love. To the degree that you place your hope in Him, to that degree He will extend His mercy to you. And it's all made possible by the death of Christ on your behalf, prompted by the amazing love of God.

Truly, what manner of love this is.

Throughout the ages to come, God shall reveal to you and me the exceeding riches of His mercy and kindness toward us through Jesus Christ. We have a lot to learn!

God loves you so much that it's going to take all of eternity for you to discover the depth of His love. His mercy is so great toward you, it will take an infinity of time to discover the depth of His mercy. Oh, the depth and the height of the riches of God's love for you and me in Christ Jesus.

Full Satisfaction

As you meditate on the staggering depth of God's love, don't neglect to ponder what that love will do for and in your own soul. God's love is not merely some fine doctrine suitable for framing—it is a truth able to make your life full and rich and deep. What satisfaction you will find in the awesome love of God.

> How precious is Your lovingkindness, O God! Therefore the children of men put their trust under the shadow of Your wings. They are abundantly satisfied with the fullness of Your house, and You give them drink from the river of Your pleasures (Psalm 36:7-8).

God is merciful, faithful, righteous, just—and filled to overflowing with lovingkindness. "How excellent is Your lovingkindness!" shouts the *King James Version*. Since God is who He is, it's proper, right and good to put your trust in Him. And for those who wisely put their trust in God, what shall happen? "They are abundantly satisfied with the fullness of Your house."

As you put your trust in your loving God, He will bless your life beyond anything you have known. You will experience for yourself the abundant satisfaction of walking in sweet fellowship with God. And then God will take it a step further—something He loves to do— "You give them drink from the river of Your pleasures." Oh the joy, the pleasure, the delight, the supreme satisfaction of serving the Lord, of living for the Lord, of walking in fellowship with God! It is sheer joy, utter pleasure, day after day.

When I think of such joy and pleasure, the Song of Solomon often comes to mind. I believe we can best appreciate this Old Testament book if we will see it as a spiritual allegory about the love that God desires to exist between Christ and His church. If we see it in that light, we will hear Christ the Groom speaking of His love for His bride: "As a lily among thorns, so is my love among the daughters" (Song of Solomon 2:2).

Christ's bride, the church, stands out against the backdrop of a world filled with darkness, sin, and thorns. Thorns, you may remember, came into the world as a result of the curse upon Adam's sin. Our world still writhes under that curse. And in that dark context, Jesus' bride stands out—His love stands out—as a lily among the thorns.

And then in the very next verse, the bride begins to respond to the love of her Bridegroom: "As an apple tree among the trees of the wood, so is my beloved among the sons. I sat down under his shadow with great delight" (2:3).

When you walk through the woods or a forest, you will find mostly nonfruit-bearing trees, yet you will see many beautiful trees and blossoms. Some trees stand out because of their size, others because of their symmetry. Still others have a glorious fragrance. But if you grow hungry and thirsty in your walk through the woods and you come upon an apple tree loaded with beautiful, luscious fruit, that tree will stand out against all the other trees. Why? Because it has the capacity to satisfy your hunger and quench your thirst.

When the bride likens her Groom to an apple tree among the trees of the woods, she declares her tree to be special. It supplies her nourishment and sustenance as well as refreshment. Her Bridegroom quenches her raging thirst.

Jesus said, "I am the bread of life. He who comes to Me shall never hunger, and he who believes in Me shall never thirst" (John 6:35). At another time He said,

> Whoever drinks of the water that I shall give him will never thirst. But the water that I shall give him will become in him a fountain of water springing up into everlasting life (John 4:14).

Jesus promises *full satisfaction* to all those who partake of Him.

Of course, such a claim is nothing new. Many in our world promise to satisfy our thirsts. New York's Madison Avenue, for example, understands fallen human nature extremely well. They know how to appeal to human desires—and one of the most powerful human desires is for happiness. Have you ever noticed how many products promise us, in one way or another, "Buying this will bring you happiness"? We see a crowd of good-looking, healthy young people laughing and enjoying life as they drink some cola. And the message insists, "All you have to do to feel this happy is to drink our brand of cola. Then you will discover life. This is the *real* reason for living; *this* is what life is all about." They leave you with the impression that if you will just purchase and use their product, your life will finally take on meaning. Your smile will gain an irresistible luster that will attract everyone to you. You will become instantly popular and you will be everything you've ever desired to be. Just use their product.

But by now you know the emptiness of such promises for happiness and satisfaction. They have no power to fulfill.

Someone once asked Ted Turner, the founder of CNN, about his success. "It's a bore," he replied. "Life is boring." When real estate mogul Donald Trump spoke with Barbara Walters, he said, "It's the chase that is exciting; the conquest is disappointing."

So it is with many things in life. It's the chase, the prospect, and the hope that excites us. But once we achieve that hope or attain that prospect, we find ourselves thirsty again. It doesn't fulfill us. It cannot bring us lasting satisfaction.

But the bride says of her Groom, "He's an apple tree among the trees of the woods. He quenches my thirst and satisfies my hunger."

When I travel abroad, I often have qualms about the drinking water. Yet something about flying tends to get me dehydrated, and so by the time I arrive I often have an aching thirst. I just cannot get enough to drink. While I usually try to take along some bottled water, I always carry a bag of apples. When I need water, I find that a good apple always quenches my thirst. And to top it off, it's very nourishing. That's why I have a special appreciation for the bride's description of her Beloved—she sees Jesus as an apple tree among the trees of the woods.

No one can satisfy the needs of your life like Jesus! No one can quench your thirst like Jesus! Only His love will do; nothing else comes close. So the bride said she sat down under the shadow of her Beloved with great delight.

Oh, how delightful it is to sit with Jesus, overshadowed by His love! Years ago we used to sing a song at church titled *Overshadowed*. Part of it said,

> How desolate my life would be, how dark and drear my nights and days, if Jesus' face I did not see to brighten all earth's ways. I'm overshadowed by His mighty love, love eternal, changeless, pure. Overshadowed by His mighty love; rest is mine, serene, secure. He died to ransom me from sin, He lives to keep me day by day. I'm overshadowed by His mighty love, love that brightens all my way.[2]

The Bible says, "He who dwells in the secret place of the Most High shall abide under the shadow of the Almighty" (Psalm 91:1). Have you come to that delightful place in life where you enjoy a close relationship with Jesus Christ, overshadowed by His limitless love? When you

2 *Overshadowed,* words and music by H.A. Ironside and George S. Schuler, 1935.

know He is there, you don't live in fear. Knowing that you're covered by His love, you don't have to worry about what tomorrow may bring. You know the Lord will be there to overshadow you, to help you.

Some shadows, of course, can create great fear. Maybe you're walking down the road by yourself at night when you pass a streetlight. Suddenly you see a second shadow beside yours. And you wonder, *Who is that? What is casting another shadow next to mine?*

But when you have come to rest under Jesus and sit safely beneath His shadow, you find great delight. The question is, have *you* found great delight in the presence of your loving Lord? Do you long to sit in His presence, feeling and experiencing His love? Can you say, along with Solomon's young bride, "Under the shadow I found great delight"?

Why Should You Believe It?

It lifts my soul to spend time thinking about God's great love for me. But you may have noticed that most of my information about the amazing love of God comes from the Bible. What if these verses about God's love are not true? What if it's all a sham?

Solomon has an important word for you. After he spent seven years building God's temple in Jerusalem, he prepared to dedicate the fabulous new structure. He told the great crowd that had gathered that day,

> The LORD said to my father David, "Whereas it was in your heart to build a temple for My name, you did well that it was in your heart. Nevertheless you shall not build the temple, but your son who will come from your body, he shall build the temple for My name." So the LORD has fulfilled His word which He spoke; and I have filled the position of my father David, and sit on the throne of Israel, as the LORD promised; and I have built a temple for the name of the LORD God of Israel (1 Kings 8:18-20).

What a testimony to the faithfulness of God in keeping His Word! God had said to Solomon's father, David, that Solomon would build the temple, and he had. And so Solomon is saying, "Look! God had made the promise to my father David, and here is proof that God keeps His promises."

The glorious temple now standing before them was the fulfillment of God's promise. God had kept His promises; the glittering temple provided the proof.

After Solomon had spoken to the people about the faithfulness of God, he turned before the altar, knelt down, lifted his hands toward heaven, and talked to God about the people. As he began his prayer of dedication, he declared,

> Lord God of Israel, there is no God in heaven above or on earth below like You, who keep Your covenant and mercy with Your servants who walk before You with all their hearts. You have kept what You promised Your servant David my father; You have both spoken with Your mouth and fulfilled it with Your hand, as it is this day (1 Kings 8:23-24).

As he finished his prayer and got up off of his knees, he turned again to the people and spoke once more about the faithfulness of God:

> Blessed be the Lord, who has given rest to His people Israel, according to all that He promised. There has not failed one word of all His good promise, which He promised through His servant Moses (1 Kings 8:56).

Almost five hundred years before, God had promised Moses that He would give the Hebrew people the land of Canaan and that He would give them peace in that land. As Solomon dedicated the temple, these descendants of Abraham found themselves dwelling safe and secure in the Promised Land. God had kept His promise; not a single word had failed.

In essence, Solomon was saying, "Folks, here it is. Four hundred and ninety years later, not a single word of God has failed. God has kept His promise. Here we are, dwelling in the land with peace and rest all around us, just as Moses declared. And today we have the sanctuary of God in our midst. Not one word has failed of all God's good promise."

Can you imagine the terrible consequences if even one word of God's promises *had* failed? If just *one* of His thousands of promises should fail, we would have to conclude that we have not heard from God, for if God speaks about some future event, then it must happen. One failure along the line—one solitary word falling short—would bring discredit to the whole field of biblical prophecy and, in fact, to the whole revelation of God. We would have to conclude that the Bible is not God's revelation to man.

But Solomon declared to the people, some five hundred years after Moses, "Not one word has failed of all that He promised."

This is why other books of religion that purport to be revelations of God stay away from specific predictions. In fact, in Isaiah's day God challenged His "rivals" to prove their divinity by foretelling the future. "If your gods are really God," the prophet suggested, "that's easy to prove. Just tell us a few things before they happen, so that when they take place we will know that they really are gods." Silence! Nothing. But then God said, "That you may know that I am God and that there is no other god like Me, I'm going to tell you what's going to happen many years in the future. After you've been carried away to Babylon for your disobedience, I will raise up a servant named Cyrus. He will set Israel free and allow My people to return from captivity." God made this bold prediction one hundred and fifty years before Cyrus was born (see Isaiah 44:28-45:13). Not one word failed of all that God spoke concerning Cyrus. Amazing!

Oh, how certain is the Word of God! You can be sure that all it predicts shall happen. You can count on it.

Of course, God has spoken in His Word not only of things that would happen in Solomon's days and in subsequent periods of Israel's ancient history, but God also has spoken of events that will take place in *our day* and in the future. Why? So that right up to this moment, we can say that not one word has failed of all that God has promised.

Concerning modern Israel, for example, God said in Ezekiel,

> But you, O mountains of Israel, you shall shoot forth your branches and yield your fruit to My people Israel, for they are about to come. For indeed I am for you, and I will turn to you, and you shall be tilled and sown (Ezekiel 36:8-9).

Ezekiel prophesied that Israel's mountains would lay desolate and barren for many long years, but that God would eventually cause the mountains to be inhabited and tilled and planted.

If you were to visit Israel today, you would see something remarkable in the Golan Heights. For centuries that area had been nothing but barren wilderness; but today you will see hundreds of acres of apple orchards, peach orchards, and various types of fruit. Or go to the hills of Naphtali, or to the areas of Sharon and Joppa. There you will see the Word of God fulfilled before your very eyes.

Go to Beersheba, which just seventy-five years ago was nothing but desert. And there, as far as your eyes can see, you will observe beautiful green fields, luscious vegetation and prolific orange trees. God said it and He has done it. *It's there*, like the garden of Eden, just as He said. It took God three thousand years to get around to it, but today you can stand there, gazing upon that modern-day garden of Eden, and you can say, "Not one word has failed of all that God promised."

Even though Israel is only about one-third the size of California—you can drive the length of the nation in a single day, and its width at some points in half an hour—yet it is the third largest fruit exporting nation in the world. Not one word has failed of all that God promised He was going to do in that land, except that which is yet future, just waiting to be done.

God so meticulously keeps His promises that *not one word* has failed—and that fact should bring either great encouragement and hope to your heart, or terror. It all depends on your relationship to God.

I am thrilled that God keeps His word so faithfully, for I know that God has promised me that if I confess with my mouth that Jesus is Lord and believe in my heart that God raised Him from the dead, I will be saved. I know God has promised that if I will confess Jesus before men, He will confess me before His Father. I also know that if I deny Him before men, He'll deny me before His Father. I know that if I receive Him, I will have eternal life, but that if I reject Him, I will face an eternity apart from Him.

Three thousand years from now—or three *million* years from now—it will still be said, "Not one word has failed of all that God has spoken." God keeps His word; you can be sure of that. It's awesome to realize that a billion years from now, either in heaven or hell, you'll be able to say, "Not one word has failed of all that God has promised."

Oh, how great is God's love for us, a love that prompted Him to send His only begotten Son to take our sin and to die in our place! May the Lord help us to understand more fully the amazing love He has for us. And may He give us a spirit of wisdom and understanding as He reveals more of Himself and His love to us.

A Song in the Night

Sometimes, despite God's tremendous love for us, we feel overwhelmed. Great billows of grief, sorrow, and trouble overflow us—and yet, even then, the Lord commands His lovingkindness in the daytime, and His song will be with us in the night. That's how great His love really is.

Several years ago I was in Pennsylvania speaking at some special services, and one night I became very sick with food poisoning. I returned to my room, with my stomach churning and burning. Oh, I was sick! I couldn't sleep at all.

As I lay there in utter misery, suddenly a beautiful worship chorus came to me. I had never heard it, but I started to sing it. And then I sang it over and over and over again. It seemed like something straight out of Psalm 42:7-8:

> Deep calls unto deep at the noise of Your waterfalls; all Your waves and billows have gone over me. The Lord will command His lovingkindness in the daytime, and in the night His song shall be with me—a prayer to the God of my life.

And so God, in His great mercy and love, gave me a beautiful song on that long night. And I thought, *This is a beautiful chorus! I had better get up and write it down. Maybe I can slip downstairs and pick out the tune on the piano, because I don't want to forget this. I want to teach this to everybody! What a neat chorus of praise and thanksgiving to worship the Lord!*

But then another thought immediately occurred to me. *If I started plunking on the piano at this hour of the night, I might awaken my host. They will think that I am either crazy, or worse. Maybe I had better not go downstairs.*

In fact, I was much too sick to get out of bed. I didn't even have the strength to turn on the light. So I just kept singing the song, over and over. And I thought, *I will **never** forget this. This is just beautiful!*

Finally, I sang myself to sleep.

When I awoke the next morning, the Lord had touched my body. He had healed me and I felt fine—except that I couldn't remember the chorus. It had left me as quickly as it had come. Oh, how I searched!

I did my best to try to remember it. I even prayed, "Oh Lord, please help me to remember that song."

But He said, "No, that was just a song for the night—*My* song to get you through a rough patch."

How big is the love of God? How much ground does it cover? It covers it all—even to the point of giving a man with a troubled stomach a beautiful song to help him through the night. What other songs does He have to give me? Who knows? But I know that His love will give me whatever I need, whenever I need it.

And His love will do the same for you.

A Love That Never Ends

FOR A LONG TIME our church dreamed of building a conference center on some choice property in California. We spent more than two years in the approval process, just trying to get a conditional use permit. I heard we might face some rough going, but that was the understatement of the year. We found the process next to impossible.

We kept a steady stream of required documents, forms, and reports flowing to the county. Some of the volumes were several inches thick. And yet the officials kept demanding more and more documentation. You wouldn't believe the mammoth bureaucracy and the never-ending red tape we faced. If I had hair, I would have pulled it all out! For the longest time I wrestled and struggled and agonized over every new development.

And I couldn't help wondering, *Lord, since this is all for You, this is for Your kingdom, You could smooth the way with a snap of Your fingers. So why don't You just start snapping?*

But no matter how often I prayed, the only thing I saw snapping was my patience. Times like these can be among the most difficult of our whole spiritual experience. We feel tremendous pressure—and God doesn't seem the slightest bit interested in doing anything about it. We pray and we plead and we claim His promises … and yet He remains silent.

Where is the love of God *then*?

Where Should You Go?

God's people have been asking questions like this for a very long time. You may even be asking similar ones right now. What should you do when life seems to scream, "Forget the love of God! It's a fantasy. You're on your own, so just grow up"?

The unidentified writer of the longest chapter in the Bible, Psalm 119, faced opposition at least as great as anything I have experienced. Out of great turmoil of heart he wrote, "They almost made an end of me on earth" (v. 87). He found himself at the edge of a cliff, wondering whether his enemies would soon toss him off. And yet he did not give up. He did not cave in to doubt. He kept forging ahead, strengthened by his confidence in God's everlasting love. How did he manage? He continued, "I did not forsake Your precepts. Revive me according to Your lovingkindness, so that I may keep the testimony of Your mouth" (v. 88). The Word of God sustained this man through his darkest hours.

So it must be with us.

When God seems silent, when He does not act immediately to remove some obstacle, correct some evil, or clear away some wrong, we must follow this man's example. When we wonder, *Lord, how long are You going to let this go on?* Or when we pray and pour out our heart to God—and yet nothing seems to improve—we need to return to the Word of God. We must go back to His unchanging promises, based upon His everlasting love, and there let our souls rest until our God moves in power at exactly the right time.

Has His Love Failed?

Tough times often prompt us to question the love of God. Very real difficulties and hardships seem at sharp odds with His promises to love us forever.

In this way, we have a lot more in common with the writers of the Bible than we sometimes think. When the psalmist found himself in terrible trouble, he cried out, "Has His mercy ceased forever? Has His promise failed forevermore? Has God forgotten to be gracious? Has He in anger shut up His tender mercies?" (Psalm 77:8-9). We all ask these painful questions at some point, usually when adversity hits, calamity arrives, or tragedy strikes.

"I am weary with my crying," David wrote, "my throat is dry; my eyes fail while I wait for my God" (Psalm 69:3).

"My eyes fail from searching Your word," said the psalmist, "saying, 'When will You comfort me?'" (Psalm 119:82).

He again pleaded with God, "Deal with Your servant according to Your mercy" (Psalm 119:124).

When you find yourself in some great distress and God seems far from your troubles, do not give up on His love. Pray as David did: "Your mercy, O LORD, endures forever; do not forsake the works of Your hands" (Psalm 138:8). David knew his share of hard times and he didn't always respond as a mature man of God should have. Like some of us at times, he wondered whether God cared at all. But eventually, he always remembered the truth; and once he did, he prayed like this:

> But You, O Lord, are a God full of compassion, and gracious, longsuffering and abundant in mercy and truth. Oh, turn to me, and have mercy on me! Give Your strength to Your servant, and save the son of Your maidservant (Psalm 86:15-16).

David did not come to God saying, "Help me because I am holy." He came to God on the only right basis; that is, on the foundation of His eternal love and abundant mercy. When trouble overwhelms you, don't come to God on the basis of your holiness, righteousness, or goodness. You might get what you deserve! Instead, come to God on the basis of His compassion, grace, mercy, truth and longsuffering.

So often we misunderstand the nature of God, especially when we feel emotionally overwhelmed. We focus on the God of wrath, vengeance, and justice—and we forget that He shows that side of His character to those who hate Him, to those who oppose Him. But to those who love Him, to those who call humbly upon His name, He displays His mercy, His grace, and His love. He is longsuffering, tender, kind, and good to all those who willingly submit their wills to His own.

So the question is, how shall we respond when we face difficulties of various kinds? When tough times come and it seems we search in vain for the love of God, what then? This is what the psalmist did when he realized that his troubles threatened to shake his confidence in God's love:

> And I said, "This is my anguish; but I will remember the years of the right hand of the Most High." I will remember the works of the Lord; surely I will remember Your wonders of old. I will also meditate on all Your work, and talk of Your deeds (Psalm 77:10-12).

Despite our feelings, God's love for us does not waver, fluctuate, or ebb and flow. His Word declares the truth: that He loves us with an everlasting love. And when our troubles multiply, we must continue to find our rest in the loving arms of God.

To a Thousand Generations

Have you ever heard a sermon on the devastation caused by "generational sin"? Preachers base their frightening comments on texts like Exodus 20:5:

> I, the LORD your God, am a jealous God, visiting the iniquity of the fathers upon the children to the third and fourth generations of those who hate Me.

Some people hear such a verse and say, "God's not fair! Why should children suffer for their parents' sin?"

Let's admit that the sins of parents often have terrible consequences upon their children. It's unavoidable. Many studies have shown, for example, that children of divorce tend to struggle in certain predictable ways, no matter how amicable the separation or how well the former partners get along with each other after the divorce. Despite any of that, their children still suffer.

Most children feel a deep sense of rejection when their dad takes off with another woman. Despite giving repeated assurances of his love, they just don't believe him. Because his actions speak louder than his words, they feel rejected and even responsible for the broken marriage. Many times, in fact, a child feels even more rejected than the wife or husband left behind. Children are the ones who generally suffer the most—and so the sins of the parents are visited upon their sons and daughters.

Of course, this doesn't mean that if you had unrighteous parents, then you must face the wrath of God for the rest of your life—because, after all, the Bible says, "He's going to visit the sins of the parents on the children to the third and fourth generations." Don't overlook the crucial condition there: "To the third and fourth generations *of those who hate Me*" (Exodus 20:5, italics added for emphasis).

If you continue in the hatred of God that your parents modeled, then God's judgment will continue, even to the third and fourth generations.

Oh, but don't stop with verse 5, as far too many preachers do. Continue reading through to Exodus 20:6, which puts the whole thing in a much more hopeful context:

> But showing mercy to thousands, to those who love Me and keep My commandments (Exodus 20:6).

While it may logically follow that a boy raised in an ungodly atmosphere is apt to grow up to be very ungodly himself, thank God for the love and grace of Jesus Christ. You can break any hurtful or wrong relationship with the past. Maybe your parents did not bring you up in the fear and admonition of the Lord; perhaps they set a very poor spiritual example. But thank God, that chain can be broken.

> Therefore, if anyone is in Christ, he is a new creation; old things have passed away; behold, all things have become new (2 Corinthians 5:17).

You don't have to suffer because of your parents' hatred of God or because of their mistakes. You can break that curse.

When Moses repeats this speech in Deuteronomy 7:9, he revises it to make his point even plainer. He says,

> Therefore know that the LORD your God, He is God, the faithful God who keeps covenant and mercy for a thousand generations with those who love Him and keep His commandments.

Do you see the stark contrast? While sin may hold sway for three or four generations in families whose parents hate God, the Lord displays His love and mercy to *a thousand generations* of those who love Him and keep His commandments.

How many generations have passed since Moses spoke these precious words from God? Let's say he lived some 3,500 years ago—although that figure is probably too large. Since most Bible scholars assign about forty years to a biblical "generation," that would mean that less than ninety generations have passed since Moses' day. So far in over three millennia—most of that time spent in heaven—Moses has experienced less than a tenth of the love and mercy that God promised him!

I know something of this blessing, since in my home both of my parents loved the Lord. They had a solid faith in Jesus Christ. God's mercy abundantly rested upon them—and God has visited His love upon their children, so that my brother and my sister walk with the Lord. We're all Christians. All four of my sister's sons are walking with the Lord; some of them are in the ministry. All of my own children love and serve the Lord; God has poured out His mercy upon them. My grandchildren love the Lord. They often talk about Jesus and His love and mercy. I have one grandson, in fact, whom I just know is going to be a preacher. He certainly has the voice for it! When he was younger, it was a little embarrassing, because whenever we went into a restaurant, everybody turned to look. He was cute as can be, but he was *loud.*

It brings back a lot of memories, because from the time I was a child, I remember my mother saying to me, "Charles, modulate your voice." Evidently I was a loud-mouthed little kid, too. So I empathize with my grandson, because he's just like his grandpa. I would be walking down the street with him or through the aisle of a toy store, and he would be singing at the top of his voice—songs about Jesus and praises to the Lord. Noisy as he was, it was a thrill to be around the little guy.

A Necessary Reminder

You cannot read too far in the Bible without running into some version of one of its most popular refrains: "Oh, give thanks to the Lord, for He is good! For His mercy endures forever."

In fact, an entire psalm was crafted around this marvelous phrase of exhortation. "Oh, give thanks to the God of heaven! For His mercy endures forever" (Psalm 136:26).

Twenty-six times in this psalm, once in each verse, the writer proclaims that "God's mercy endures forever." Now, why did God inspire the author to repeat this truth so often? He did it for emphasis, that it might get implanted deep in our hearts and embedded firmly in our minds. Never, ever, *ever* should we question whether God will be merciful enough to forgive us our sins and pardon our transgressions. His mercy endures forever! His love is without limit! His love will cover you always! In fact, in all situations and under all circumstances, *God's mercy endures forever*. You need this truth as much as I do.

Psalm 118 is the last of the "Hallel psalms," which faithful Jews sang on their journeys of pilgrimage to Jerusalem. As Jesus made His way to Jerusalem for the Day of Atonement, this would have been the last song on His "must sing" list. For centuries interpreters recognized it as a messianic psalm, a prophecy about the coming Messiah. So as Jesus sang this psalm with His disciples, just hours before His arrest and crucifixion, He knew very well that portions of it referred directly to Him.

I wonder, how would it be to sing such a psalm knowing that it's talking specifically about *you*? Jesus knew everything that awaited Him in Jerusalem. He knew of Judas' treachery. He knew His disciples would desert Him. He knew Peter would deny Him. He knew He would be arrested, falsely accused, condemned to death, beaten, mocked, tortured, and finally crucified. So, knowing all that, can you see why His loving Father would fortify His soul with the words of Psalm 118?

> Oh, give thanks unto the Lord, for He is good. For His mercy endures forever. Let Israel now say, "His mercy endures forever." Let the house of Aaron now say, "His mercy endures forever." Let those who fear the Lord now say, "His mercy endures forever" (Psalm 118:1-4).

Jesus recognized that in just a few hours He would become "the Lamb of God who takes away the sin of the world" (John 1:29). He would "become sin" for us all (2 Corinthians 5:21). He would bear our sins in His own body on the tree and through His stripes He would heal us (1 Peter 2:24). And surely the goodness of God was manifested in the words of Psalm 118, assuring our Savior of God's eternal love for Him. In our Lord's darkest hour, God ministered to Him through the truth of His eternal Word: *"His mercy endures forever!"*

God's Love Disciplines

God always deals with His children in love, even though sometimes He must inflict pain in order to keep them in line—or get them back in line. The Bible insists, however, that God never inflicts pain willingly. In a sense, you might say that God is a lenient disciplinarian. He'll let you get by with an awful lot before He really comes down on you.

The prophet Jeremiah wrote,

> For the LORD will not cast off forever. Though He causes grief, yet He will show compassion according to the multitude of His mercies. For He does not afflict willingly, nor grieve the children of men (Lamentations 3:31-33).

God doesn't strike willingly!

When I was growing up, just before my dad disciplined me, he used to say, "Son, this hurts me worse than it hurts you." I never believed him. I thought, *Come on! Who are you trying to kid?* I thought it was just a line—until I became a parent myself, and then I understood. When I had to administer proper and appropriate punishment for my children's misdeeds, it really did hurt me worse than it hurt them. In the same way, God never afflicts His children willingly. He shows us compassion "according to the multitude of His mercies." Whatever He does, He always does in love.

"But if He *really* loved us," someone says, "He would never strike at all." Such a perspective reveals a serious case of spiritual amnesia. For the Bible replies,

> And you have forgotten the exhortation which speaks to you as to sons: "My son, do not despise the chastening of the LORD, nor be discouraged when you are rebuked by Him; for whom the LORD loves He chastens, and scourges every son whom He receives" (Hebrews 12:5-6).

From the Bible's perspective, *the failure* to discipline reveals a lack of love. God demonstrates His love for His children when He disciplines, in love, those who stand in need of it. That is why we hear Jesus saying, "As many as I love, I rebuke and chasten. Therefore be zealous and repent" (Revelation 3:19). And that's why we hear the apostle Paul saying to the carnal believers of ancient Corinth, "What do you want? Shall I come to you with a rod, or in love and a spirit of gentleness?" (1 Corinthians 4:21).

When God disciplines us, He does so out of love. He wants to bless us, not blast us. God does not delight in judgment. He would much rather show mercy than judgment. As He said through the prophet, "I have no pleasure in the death of the wicked" (Ezekiel 33:11). God wants to show us His mercy and demonstrate His grace. That is why He is so slow to exercise judgment.

And to be honest, sometimes I wish He weren't.

A lot of people fill the earth with their filth, condemning other men's souls and exerting a rotten influence upon our children. I'd like to snuff them out, *right now!* Sometimes, God's patience seems like a big problem to me. "God, why do You let them get by with that? Why do You let them do that? Lord, why don't You just smite them?" God delays His judgment because He wants to give everyone every possible opportunity to turn from their evil—chance after chance after chance.

Still, there is a limit, even to the patience of God.

> The LORD is merciful and gracious, slow to anger, and abounding in mercy. Nevertheless, He will not always strive with us, nor will He keep His anger forever (Psalm 103:8-9).

The prophets speak of the day when the cup of His indignation will overflow—and then *watch out!*

Don't misinterpret God's patience as evidence that He doesn't know or doesn't see the evil you do. He *does* see—and what He sees pains Him greatly. But He loves you and thus He remains patient with you. Never imagine that God approves of your sin simply because He has let you get by with it, so far. God can never support evil or sin. But He *is* merciful. He *is* slow to anger, of great kindness, and He doesn't want to bring pain into your life. He doesn't want to bring His judgment—so don't force Him to do so.

God is so merciful that He often forestalls His judgment. You may deserve to be wiped out by God. You might be worthy of His most terrible judgment. But God is so merciful that if you'll just call upon Him and seek Him with all of your heart, He will forgive you. His kindness and love make Him reluctant to bring judgment.

Nevertheless, don't mistake *reluctance* for *refusal.* God has made His stance very clear in several places in His Word, among them:

> If they break My statutes and do not keep My commandments, then I will punish their transgression with the rod, and their iniquity with stripes (Psalm 89:31-32).

Still, even in tough passages like this one, He reveals His tender heart:

> Nevertheless My lovingkindness I will not utterly take from him, nor allow My faithfulness to fail. My covenant I will not break, nor alter the word that has gone out of My lips (Psalm 89:33-34).

Perhaps the best way to respond to this is to remember the message of Psalm 103:17, which says, "The mercy of the LORD is from everlasting to everlasting on those who fear Him." Who can expect His mercy? Those who *fear* Him, who never forget that He is the great King above all kings, the Creator of the universe and the Judge of all the earth. How important it is that we live in proper respect and reverence for God.

I worry a bit about this "good ol' Buddy upstairs" attitude that seems so prevalent today. We have an awesome privilege to fellowship with the eternal, holy and righteous God. He is the One who made it possible for us to live with Him forever through faith in His Son, Jesus Christ. We need to maintain a proper respect and reverence for God, whose "mercy is from everlasting to everlasting upon those who fear Him."

Love in the Ruins

Personal trials, tragedies, and even divine discipline can all prompt us to doubt God's everlasting love. Even those of us who have walked with the Lord for many years sometimes feel tempted to think He has abandoned us, especially when we walk through the rubble of lives destroyed by disobedience.

The man we know as "the weeping prophet," Jeremiah, came to feel this way. Jeremiah had just lived through one of the worst disasters ever to befall God's people. The Babylonians had descended upon the Hebrew nation and devastated it. Whomever they did not kill, they locked in chains and led away into captivity. They left only the poorest of the land behind to remain in their own ruined shacks.

In this depressed, bitter state, Jeremiah poured out his broken heart, recording his dark experiences in the little book of Lamentations. For three chapters he mourns and wails, freely expressing his deep anguish. And then, suddenly, in the middle of the book, he has a radical change of mind. Rather than continuing to recall the bitterness and horror of the murderous siege, he allows his thoughts to bring him home. He begins to think of the Lord—and first of all—the Lord's mercies:

> Through the Lord's mercies we are not consumed, because His compassions fail not. They are new every morning; great is Your faithfulness (Lamentations 3:22-23).

It's as if the prophet thought, *I am still here. I'm still alive. Where there is life, there is hope—and if it weren't for God's mercies, I would long ago have been destroyed. I would have been consumed in that dreadful siege. Things really could be worse. God has been compassionate toward me. He has dealt with me in faithfulness and in love.*

Jeremiah had been thinking that God had forsaken him completely. "God has hedged me in," he said in essence. "He's not listening to my prayers." But when he stopped long enough to adjust his thinking along more biblical lines, he quickly reaffirmed the truth: God's love never fails.

God will never stop loving those who belong to Him. That means God never has stopped—and never will stop—loving you. He does not love you when you behave and hate you when you disobey. God's love for you always remains constant and unchanging. It never fails. God continually pours out His love upon you—and that love depends not upon what you are, but upon who He is. As Jeremiah finally recalled, *His compassions fail not; they are new every morning.*

No Alterations

Shakespeare once wrote, "Love is not love which alters when it alteration finds." He was right. Genuine love remains constant. When it doesn't, you know you're dealing with something other than true love.

"Oh, how I love you," a man tells his date. "You're my dream come true! I'd swim the Pacific Ocean to be by your side. I'd fly to the moon to be close to you. In fact, until the world stops turning and the stars flame out, I … uh … what's that smell? Yikes! You have bad breath. *Sorry*, but I've changed my mind."

Love is not love which alters when it alteration finds.

When we look for a spouse, too often we have a mental image of the perfect man or woman, our "ideal mate." And so when we "fall in love," we do not fall in love with them, but we fall in love with our dream. And when they don't meet up to our impossible standards, then we're no longer in love.

That's ridiculous. That means only that we never were in love to begin with. Love is not love which alters when it alteration finds.

That is why true love is so hard to find among humankind. No wonder the Bible says, "Many a man claims to have unfailing love, but a faithful man who can find?" (Proverbs 20:6, *NIV*). True love, genuine love—the real deal—can be found consistently only with God.

Our Lord is never deceived by an idealization. You cannot fool Him with your smooth, suave manners or your genteel, gallant ways. You cannot deceive Him even a little. He knew what a rascal you were from the beginning.

But still He loves you. That's the amazing thing. And for God to know you as thoroughly as He does, and yet still love you, is one of the greatest miracles of all. *God never stops loving you.*

Give It to Him

When the pressure is on and it seems as if you will be swallowed up by some calamity—when you've been waiting and waiting and nothing at all appears to be happening—you may feel tempted to give up on any divine response or action. But then the Spirit leads you back to the Word of God and once more you recall the faithfulness of God to His promises.

And that is where your soul finds rest.

"God," you say, "it is in Your loving hands. You are just going to have to take care of it. I cannot do it. I'm going to trust in You."

Of course, people will always try to get you back in the middle of it. They'll do their best to scare you, although usually not on purpose. Don't let them. Enjoy that beautiful rest, knowing that your problem is in the hands of your loving Lord, come what may.

So what if the whole thing collapses? So what if it all goes down the tubes? Hey, it's in His hands. If God wants it to go down the tubes, then how can you stop it anyway?

But so long as you strive to see that your own will gets done, you'll wrestle with it and groan under its weight and endure all kinds of mental turmoil. You'll insist, "God, You need to do it my way, or else!" I'm telling you; you will have no rest as long as you insist that God sees things your way and does things your way. But when you finally say, "Lord, I know You love me. So You just do it. You just take care of it the way You know is best. You do what You want to do," then you can kick back and say, "Well, it's in His hands. God's going to take care of it, one way or another."

Remember the story that began this chapter about my trying to get the county to approve a conference center that our church wanted to build? I was just grinding over this issue until I finally came to the place where I said, "Lord, it's Your problem. I know You love me. I know You love Your church. So it's Your problem from here on out."

Thank God He brought me to a place of patience. Through this incident He taught me a great lesson: "tribulation worketh patience" (Romans 5:3, *KJV*). Tribulation and dealing with recalcitrant county officials has worked patience in my heart. I'm not striving with it anymore. It's in the Lord's loving hands.

Okay, but when are you going to have your next hearing? I would think. To tell you the truth, while we were waiting for the next hearing to take place, a better piece of property that had been a Boy Scouts' camp became available, in a much more desirable location and in a more heavily forested area. It was much closer to the church, already zoned for a camp, and more suited in every way for our needs. We bought this site instead and have built a beautiful camp that has ministered to over a quarter of a million children. We saw the hand of God's love revealed through this recalcitrant planning commission, who were putting us through so much time and grief until the other property became available.

As the psalmist wrote in Psalm 73:26, "My flesh and my heart fail but God is the strength of my heart and my portion forever." And I rest in my heavenly Father, "who has loved us and given us everlasting consolation and good hope by grace" (2 Thessalonians 2:16).

Believe me, it's a good place to rest. And there's more than enough room for you, too.

Two Testaments, One Story

SO OFTEN THESE DAYS we hear people talking about the God of the Old Testament versus the God of the New Testament, as though the Bible presents us with two separate and distinct Gods. One, they say, is an awesome, fierce, angry, Mount Sinai-law-giving, fire and judgment-breathing God; the other is a "turn the other cheek," "bless those that curse you," and "love covers a multitude of sins" God, as manifested by Jesus.

These folks tend to portray the God of the Old Testament as mean, cruel and vicious. He's stern—just very, very heavy. On the other hand, they depict the God of the New Testament as syrupy-sweet, liquid love.

"Oh, I don't believe in the God of the Old Testament," they may say. "He's all wrath, judgment, and vengeance. I much prefer the

New Testament God. I believe in a God of love and forgiveness and kindness."

In reality, of course, Scripture presents only *one* God, not two. From cover to cover, the Bible clearly shows us one God with two primary sides to His nature. Thank God He is loving and gracious and merciful—the Old Testament, by the way, reveals Him as such! But He is also a holy and righteous God who brings judgment upon the ungodly—and the New Testament reveals Him as such.

The Bible presents us with one God who, in His great love, sent His only begotten Son into the world to die for our sins so that He might rescue us from the terrible judgment we deserved. Never allow yourself to fall for this "Old Testament God" versus "New Testament God" blasphemy! The God of the Old Testament *is* the God of the New Testament—and that is precisely why we can completely depend upon the salvation He offers.

God Doesn't Change

What if there really were a difference between the Old Testament God and the New Testament God? What if God really did change over time? Would that be good news for us?

Not in a million years. In fact, it would be the worst news imaginable.

If God changed with the passing of time, He might easily promise us one thing today and renege on His commitment tomorrow. We couldn't rely on anything He said. We could place no confidence in His Word. So I rejoice when I hear the Bible say,

> God is not a man, that He should lie, nor a son of man, that He should repent. Has He said, and will He not do? Or has He spoken, and will He not make it good? (Numbers 23:19).

The Scripture insists on the faithfulness of God—that He will certainly fulfill *all* of His promises to us—based on His unchanging nature.

Toward the very end of the Old Testament, in fact, it is the fixed character of God that God Himself calls upon to assure us that He will save us, just as He promised: "For I am the Lord, I do not change; therefore you are not consumed, O sons of Jacob" (Malachi 3:6). If God *did* change, then we would have something to worry about. But since He does not, He will surely keep His word to save all those who come to Him in faith.

The prophet Malachi did not invent this idea. Centuries before his day, an unidentified author wrote to God,

> Of old You laid the foundation of the earth, and the heavens are the work of Your hands. They will perish, but You will endure; yes, they will all grow old like a garment; like a cloak You will change them, and they will be changed. But You are the same, and Your years will have no end (Psalm 102:25-27).

One New Testament writer considered this passage so important that he quoted it approvingly (Hebrews 1:10-12).

Another New Testament writer, James, called God the "Father of lights" and assured us that with Him "there is no variation or shadow of turning" (James 1:17). The Bible also calls Jesus the "brightness" of God's glory and "the express image of His person" and then insists, "Jesus Christ is the same yesterday, today, and forever" (Hebrews 1:3, 13:8). Like Father, like Son.

Be very, *very* glad that God never changes!

Jesus' Take on God

Most people who reject a grumpy "Old Testament God" in favor of a nicer "New Testament God" cite Jesus Christ as a major reason for their perspective. Somehow they see Jesus and what He stands for as strongly opposing the Old Testament's picture of God.

It makes me wonder: Have they ever actually *read* what Jesus said and did?

Throughout the Gospels, Jesus puts Himself in complete alignment with God as He is revealed in the Old Testament. He never says, "I'm so sorry, but the Bible got it wrong. Let Me set the record straight." While He frequently challenges practices and images of God that had become distorted over time, He never once claims to present a picture of His heavenly Father that opposes Scripture in any way. Much to the contrary!

Jesus most often used the word "Father" to refer to God. The question is, did He have a different Father in mind than the God presented in the Old Testament? We get a big clue in Mark 12:26 (also Matthew 22:32 and Luke 20:37). There He unambiguously refers to His Father as "the God of Abraham, Isaac and Jacob"—in other words, the God of the Old Testament.

One day some Sadducees confronted Jesus. The Sadducees were a materialistic sect of Jews who had rejected all of the Old Testament, except for the five books of Moses. They knew that Jesus had taught about the resurrection of the dead, a doctrine which they did not accept. You could often hear them saying things like, "Nowhere in the books of Moses does God teach immortality or resurrection! All that stuff came along later with the prophets. Nothing in the Pentateuch endorses any such idea."

So when they challenged Jesus on this issue, the Master took them to their own turf, the Pentateuch. "Are you therefore not mistaken," Jesus asked them, "because you do not know the Scriptures nor the power of God?" (Mark 12:24). And then He immediately hit them with this bombshell:

> But concerning the dead, that they rise, have you not read in the book of Moses, in the burning bush passage, how God spoke to him, saying, "I am the God of Abraham, the God of Isaac, and the God of Jacob"? He is not the God of the dead, but the God of the living. You are therefore greatly mistaken (Mark 12:26-27).

Using the Sadducees' own "authorized" book of Moses as His proof text, Jesus set the record straight. And at the same time, He endorsed the God we see portrayed in the earliest books of the Old Testament—that is, the God of Abraham, the God of Isaac, and the God of Jacob. *That* is the God He came to reveal. *That* is the God whose will He had come to do. And that is the God He consistently called "Father."

Jesus insisted that He had come to do the works of His Father, as prophesied in the Old Testament Scriptures: "The Son can do nothing of Himself, but what He sees the Father do; for whatever He does, the Son also does in like manner" (John 5:19).

He maintained that He spoke the very words of the Father: "Whatever I speak, just as the Father has told Me, so I speak" (John 12:50).

Certainly He never claimed to announce a God different from the one revealed in the Old Testament:

> Do not think that I came to destroy the Law or the Prophets. I did not come to destroy but to fulfill. For assuredly, I say to you, till heaven and earth pass away, one jot or one tittle will by no means pass from the law till all is fulfilled (Matthew 5:17-18).

Nor did He want anyone to believe that God loved humankind only because Jesus had twisted the Holy One's arm:

> For the Father Himself loves you, because you have loved Me, and have believed that I came forth from God (John 16:27).

In fact, Jesus came to earth to die for our sins because the Father had sent Him:

> For I have come down from heaven, not to do My own will, but the will of Him who sent Me. This is the will of the Father who sent Me, that of all He has given Me I should lose nothing, but should raise it up at the last day. And this is the will of Him who sent Me, that everyone who sees the Son and believes in Him may have everlasting life (John 6:38-40).

To put it succinctly, Jesus said He had come to make known the Father: "He who has seen Me has seen the Father" (John 14:9). Our Savior did not come to reveal to us a God different from the one pictured from Genesis to Malachi; He came so that we could see the God of the Old Testament "in the flesh," up close and personal in the amazing person of Jesus Christ.

The Old Testament: Love and Justice

One remarkable day Moses asked to see the glory of God. He was really asking to see a more complete picture of his Lord—he wanted a glimpse of God's real nature, of His true character. Amazingly, God granted His humble servant's request. And so He placed Moses in a cleft of a rock and then passed by, proclaiming His name:

> The Lord, the Lord God, merciful and gracious, longsuffering, and abounding in goodness and truth, keeping mercy for thousands, forgiving iniquity and transgression and sin (Exodus 34:6-7).

Now surely this should put to rest the myth that there are really two Gods revealed in the Bible, the God of the Old Testament and the God of the New. How does God proclaim Himself in this second book of the Bible? He is a God full of mercy, gracious, longsuffering, abounding in goodness and in truth. These are the marvelous characteristics of God declared throughout the Old Testament.

Hundreds of years after Moses' time, the prophet Isaiah would look back to the time of the exodus and proclaim,

> I will mention the lovingkindnesses of the Lord, according to all that the Lord has bestowed upon us, and the great goodness toward the house of Israel, which He has bestowed on them according to His mercies, according to the multitude of His lovingkindnesses (Isaiah 63:7).

Staggered by the goodness of his Lord, Isaiah takes a deep breath and then remembers afresh how God has treated His people:

> In all their affliction He was afflicted, and the Angel of His Presence saved them; in His love and in His pity He redeemed them; and He bore them and carried them all the days of old (v. 9).

What a beautiful Scripture! "In all their affliction He was afflicted." The early disciples recognized that whatever persecutions they faced, they faced for Jesus Christ. So when the religious authorities beat them and commanded them not to preach anymore in the name of Jesus, they went their way, praising the Lord that they had been accounted worthy to suffer persecution for Jesus' sake (Acts 5:41).

Whenever you endure any persecution for the name of the Lord, remember that in all of your afflictions He is afflicted. He bears your sorrow. He shares with you the afflictions, the tribulations, the persecutions—and He always has. That is the unchanging heart of the Lord Almighty for His children.

Even before Moses had taken a single step toward leading the nation of Israel out of Egyptian slavery, God had told him,

> I have surely seen the oppression of My people who are in Egypt, and have heard their cry because of their taskmasters, for I know their sorrows (Exodus 3:7).

In His love and in His pity, God redeemed the enslaved Hebrews from the harsh treatment of the Egyptians. And not only that, but "He bore them and carried them all the days of old." Through that entire agonizing wilderness experience, the Lord stayed with His people. He protected them, He watched over them and He preserved them—and not because He had to, but because that is what His tender heart of love moved Him to do.

Many generations later, Nehemiah counted on the love and mercy of God when he felt called by God to do something about the deplorable conditions in Jerusalem following the Babylonian exile. He knew that the judgment of God had finally fallen on his nation due to the people's stubbornness and rebellion. He recognized that his countrymen had angered God by their disobedience and insulted God through their idol worship. He knew they had it coming ever since they left Egypt centuries before. And yet he also knew something else:

> They [our fathers] refused to obey, and they were not mindful of Your wonders that You did among them. But they hardened their necks, and in their rebellion they appointed a leader to return to their bondage. But You are God, ready to pardon, gracious and merciful, slow to anger, abundant in kindness, and did not forsake them (Nehemiah 9:17).

Nehemiah confessed that spiritual failure had characterized his people ever since the exodus—and yet he could still say, "God, You're gracious. You're ready to pardon. You're merciful and patient. And I know that You have not forsaken us as our sins deserve." Isn't that beautiful? That sounds like it could have come straight from the pen of Paul as he described the grace of God in the New Testament. Oh, how gracious is God! How merciful and understanding and pardoning!

The New Testament: Justice and Love

Those who think that the God of the New Testament is all forgiveness, kindness, patience, sweetness and universal salvation for everybody—regardless of their commitment to Jesus Christ—had better reread several large portions of the last twenty-seven books of the Bible. If they read a bit more carefully, they'll find out that He is also a God of judgment. Those who rebel against Him and set their heart against Him will one day have to face a day of terrible judgment. And who will be able to stand?

The New Testament frequently speaks of the wrath of God. Listen to Paul: "For the wrath of God is revealed from heaven against all ungodliness and unrighteousness of men, who suppress the truth in unrighteousness" (Romans 1:18). The apostle then further describes the coming judgment of God.

The writer of Hebrews says,

> Therefore we must give the more earnest heed to the things we have heard, lest we drift away. For if the word spoken through angels proved steadfast, and every transgression and disobedience received a just reward, how shall we escape if we neglect so great a salvation? … For we know Him who said, "Vengeance is Mine, I will repay," says the Lord. And again, "The Lord will judge His people" (Hebrews 2:1-3, 10:30).

Jesus Christ demonstrated grace and truth, but to those who reject that grace and truth there remains:

> A certain fearful expectation of judgment and fiery indignation, which will devour the adversaries. Anyone who has rejected Moses' law dies without mercy on the testimony of two or three witnesses. Of how much worse punishment, do you suppose, will he be thought worthy who has trampled the Son of God underfoot, counted the blood of the covenant by which he was sanctified a common thing, and insulted the Spirit of grace? … It is a fearful thing to fall into the hands of the living God … For our God is a consuming fire (Hebrews 10:27-29, 31; 12:29).

Remember, that wasn't the prophet Jeremiah thundering out fearful threats! That was the writer of the book of Hebrews, declaring the judgment of God that shall come upon those who reject His grace and mercy through Jesus Christ.

The final book of the New Testament, Revelation, fixes an almost blinding spotlight on the wrath and justice of God. It predicts the response of ungodly men caught in the crosshairs of God's judgment:

> And the kings of the earth, the great men, the rich men, the commanders, the mighty men, every slave and every free man, hid themselves in the caves and in the rocks of the mountains, and said to the mountains and rocks, "Fall on us and hide us from the face of Him who sits on the throne and from the wrath of the Lamb! For the great day of His wrath has come, and who is able to stand?" (Revelation 6:15-17).

Oh yes, God is a God of love. He is longsuffering, full of compassion, merciful, gracious and patient. Thank God for that! But He is also a God of righteous judgment and unblinking holiness. He is both. And He always has been.

The Love in God's Judgment

I must say, though, that even in God's justice, He displays His love. In love, God warns us against destructive decisions and activities. He seeks to protect us from our fallen nature, which is bent toward the things that can destroy us.

Certain activities carry a certain, built-in judgment. If you do certain ungodly things, then as a natural consequence you are going to suffer certain nasty repercussions. Whatever a man sows, that he will also reap (Galatians 6:7). Particular activities and actions automatically bring corresponding consequences.

As you study God's laws as given in Scripture, you see that, in essence, God prohibited destructive choices—choices that are destructive to your health, to your relationship with your spouse, with your family, with your friends, and destructive to your relationship with God. He outlawed those things that naturally destroy you. On the other hand, He mandated the things that build you up, that make you a better person and enhance your relationships with others and magnify your relationship with God.

So you cannot fault the law of God. "The law of the Lord is perfect," the Bible says, "converting the soul: the testimony of the Lord is sure, making wise the simple" (Psalm 19:7). You cannot fault God's law—and yet we often rebel against it. My flesh wants to do things that God's law prohibits, the things that by their very nature destroy me. And if I do those things despite what God tells me, I'm going to suffer the inevitable consequences of my rebellion. And so God warns us in His Word that if we do this, then that will happen. He plainly warns us of the consequences of violating His law—and He does so because He is gracious, not because He isn't.

I can often do destructive things—and yet God remains compassionate. He sees me in my turmoil. He sees me in my sorrow. He sees me in my grief. He wants me to avoid the things that would destroy me—and He even helps me to avoid them—but I can rebel. I choose to do them anyhow. And so I suffer the consequences.

Even then, however, God is gracious and merciful and full of compassion: "Oh, you poor little child; why would you do that?" He seems to say. And then He reaches down, lifts me out of the pit and sets me on my feet again.

Have you ever had to sit back and watch one of your children make a serious mistake? I think that has to be one of the most frustrating things parents ever have to face.

When young adults reach an age when they start making their own decisions, and you see them about to make a choice that you know is wrong and destructive, your heart breaks. You know their decision is going to bring them pain and hurt. And so you do your best to keep them from it. You do everything you possibly can, within the limits of the law. You want to prevent them from injuring or destroying themselves. You want to spare them the terrible pain and sorrow you know is coming. You want so desperately to shield them from all of that—but sometimes they get headstrong. They get stubborn and rebellious and they act against your good judgment, against your pleas, against your advice and counsel and even threats. They go ahead with their plan and there's not one thing you can do to stop them.

You just have to stand by and wait for the awful cycle to complete itself.

When their plans blow up and you find them in horrible pain—the very agony you wanted to spare them from—you step in to pick up the pieces and to help them put their life back together. If only they had listened, they could have avoided all of that!

It's excruciating to watch your children make serious mistakes, despite your counsel and warnings. You can see what they cannot—the destruction and excruciating pain that will surely follow.

I think tough situations like these give us some insight into God's experience with us. He sees us doing ungodly things that He knows are going to bring us pain. They invite suffering. And so He does everything short of violating our will to dissuade us from our foolish choices. He wants us to change. But we get stubborn and headstrong and so we go ahead and do what we want anyhow.

Then He just waits.

When we arrive at the crushing part of the story, the painful part, He comes to us once more, full of compassion. He is so gracious and He helps us to put together the broken pieces. Had we only obeyed and listened to Him, He would have helped us to avoid the whole ugly scene.

Even though we do foolish things in our own headstrong will that bring us pain and hurt, God remains gracious, full of compassion, slow to anger and full of great mercy. In other words, when we go ahead and do something stupid despite His Word, He doesn't just cut us off and say, "All right, that's enough. I've had it with you! Forget you; I disown you. Never call on Me again!"

You don't do that with your children, do you? You feel their pain and hurt; and then, at the right time, you help them pick up the pieces and put everything back together. God is just like that. Even when He disciplines us, even when He has to chastise members of His church, He does so with compassion, grace and love. Even in God's justice, He displays great love. But why suffer terrible pain and deep sorrow when you don't have to?

My Personal Journey to Love

As I have mentioned before, I grew up in a very godly Christian home.

I believed in Jesus Christ from day one. From the time I was thirteen days old, my parents carried me to church. I slept in the pews and grew up in a God-honoring environment.

Yet, as all teenagers must, I came to a place in my spiritual growth and development where I had to create my own relationship with God. I had to develop a spiritual foundation and work through a personal theology. You might say I had to construct my own house of faith in the Lord.

As I moved through that period, being challenged intellectually by my studies—especially my philosophy and biology classes—I came to a short period when I questioned *everything.* I even began to question the existence of God. I wondered if I really believed in Him at all.

Maybe there is something to atheism, I thought. *Maybe all this spiritual stuff is nothing more than the creation of man.* I went through a period of real misery, almost sinking from the weight of my oppressive thoughts. *Maybe God doesn't exist. Maybe it is all man's concepts and ideas, since man appears to need to believe in* ***something.*** The more I entertained thoughts like these, the more I sank emotionally. And then I thought, *Maybe God doesn't exist—but it's easier to believe that He does exist than to believe that He doesn't.* As I looked at the world and the universe, I found it much easier to believe in the existence of God than to believe that everything I saw came into being by sheer chance. If you don't believe in the existence of God, then you have a lot of explaining to do!

How can you see? How can you hear? How can you walk? How can you feel? How can you remember? Can you really have all of these capacities just by random, blind chance? Not believing in God left too many unanswered questions for me.

My belief in God strengthened as I observed creation. As I studied nature, I saw design and purpose everywhere. I saw delicate balances in nature. I noticed the oxygen/nitrogen cycles. I saw crucial water/dry land proportions, two-thirds to one-third. So it became easier for me to say, "Okay, I believe in God."

You may say, "Well, Chuck, that's not much in the way of proof." And in one way, you'd be right. But in another way, if you're sinking, then it's awfully reassuring to feel your foot landing upon something solid! So I thought, *Yes, I do believe in God.*

But I couldn't stop there. How could I stop with a limited belief in the existence of God? I had already seen that creation seemed to reveal a consistent divine design and purpose. I reasoned that all of these delicate systems and necessary balances existed because they were required for man's existence—and if God had a design and a purpose for all created things, then He also must have a design and a purpose for me.

But if God had a purpose for me, then what was it? Why had God designed *me*?

There I ran into another problem. With so many religions in the world, how could anyone identify the true God? That was the next step I had to take toward building my own faith and relationship with God.

And so for a time I studied Judaism, Islam, and Buddhism. I also began to make a serious study of the Bible. If God did exist, I reasoned, and if He had created me for a purpose, then He must have revealed Himself to humankind early in history. And of necessity, He would have to perpetuate that revelation to the present day. Therefore, I immediately rejected all the religious systems of the past that had fallen by the wayside. I didn't bother to look into Greek or Roman mythology or other religions that had long ago made their way into history's dustbin. If any of them were *true*, that would be an admission that God could not keep the required revelation alive to the present time—and that would suggest that God had no interest in modern man, that He didn't care what happens to us today. Clearly, that option was unacceptable.

For a similar reason I also rejected the new religions that have made their appearance in relatively recent times. I dismissed the "prophets" who claimed to have received some "true revelation" of God, hidden for ages until the world found itself blessed by this prophet. I therefore quickly rejected all modern cults, because they essentially condemn all men and women who died before the new "prophet" arrived, as if God didn't care about them but for some reason had suddenly taken an interest in the human race. I just couldn't buy that idea. I reasoned that any genuine revelation of God had to begin early in history and had to continue to the present day. That's why I chose just these faiths to study: Judaism, Islam, Buddhism, and Christianity.

But the more I studied, the more I became convinced that the Bible alone was indeed the genuine revelation of God. I saw that it stands separate, apart, distinct—and in many cases, in direct opposition to the religious systems of man. It appeared to me that while religious systems represented human attempts to reach out to God, Christianity was God's attempt to reach human beings. Religion tried to show men how to become good enough to be accepted by God; Christianity alone claimed that no sinful human could ever be good enough to be accepted by God. It alone focused on trusting exclusively in the grace of God. It bypassed the whole idea of a system of saving works and said instead, "You can do nothing to be worthy of God. You can only receive His grace, His love and His mercy, extended to you through His crucified and risen Son, Jesus Christ."

In addition, the more I read of the Bible, the more fascinated I became with its prophetic aspects. I learned that the Bible itself declares fulfilled prophecy to be the built-in proof of its divine origin. God tells us about specific events before they happen, so that when they occur we might know He is God and there is no one else like Him (see Isaiah 44:7-8). Jesus repeatedly spoke in this way to His disciples:

> And now I have told you before it comes, that when it does come to pass, you may believe (John 14:29; see also Matthew 24:25; Mark 13:23; John 16:4).

Today I have no doubts, no qualms, no reservations about the unique, divine origin of the Bible, or about faith in Jesus Christ as the only road to a dynamic relationship with God. Today I know what the apostle Paul meant when he wrote,

> For as many as are led by the Spirit of God, these are sons of God. For you did not receive the spirit of bondage again to fear, but you received the Spirit of adoption by whom we cry out, "Abba, Father." The Spirit Himself bears witness with our spirit that we are children of God (Romans 8:14-16).

The most important thing in the world for anyone to discover is the true and living God for himself or herself. It's vitally important that you know who God is. And the only absolutely reliable guide you'll find anywhere is the Bible—both Old and New Testaments.

He Is All

In the Old Testament we encounter a God of grace and mercy, a long-suffering God who offers to forgive all the truly repentant. At the same time we observe a holy God who can never merely wink at sin.

In the New Testament we find a righteous God of judgment and wrath, but one who urges us in love to escape the wrath to come through faith in Jesus Christ.

They are one and the same God. There isn't one God of the Old Testament and a different God of the New Testament. People may read into the Bible what they want, but in reality both Testaments reveal God as gracious, loving, kind, merciful, and forgiving. And in both Testaments we see Him as a God of judgment and wrath, who by no means will clear the guilty—that is, without genuine repentance. God never says to anyone, "Well, you seem like a nice enough person. I know you're trying! You're forgiven." Jesus emphasized repeatedly, "unless you repent you will all likewise perish" (Luke 13:3, 5).

God is a God of love—yes! He is a God of mercy—yes! He is a compassionate God, a merciful and gracious God—yes! A good God—yes! He is also a God of justice—correct! A God of judgment—correct again!

Our loving Lord is all that the Bible declares Him to be. And Scripture says that He longs for you to enjoy a vital, growing relationship with Him, and discover for yourself all that He is.

The Purpose of His Coming

IT HAPPENS EVERY YEAR. As the calendar approaches its last page, interesting things start taking place. People begin clearing out a special spot somewhere in their homes to put up a tree (living or artificial). Colored lights get strung high on buildings, sparkling in the night sky. Fat men in red suits appear almost everywhere, while commercial radio stations play tunes you simply don't hear during any other time of year.

Christmas is coming.

As this is being written, the Christmas season once more is in full swing. For believers in Christ, the season means much more than tinsel and presents and nostalgic viewings of classic holiday movies. We remember the nativity, the little babe lying in the manger as shepherds look on in adoration. The virgin has brought forth her firstborn son—Emmanuel, "God with us."

Why did Jesus come that first Christmas? While the Bible gives many reasons for His advent, one of the most basic purposes was to reveal to the world the truth about God. Jesus' heavenly Father sent His Son into this world to give us a firsthand, totally accurate revelation of the only true and eternal God.

The Exact Image of God's Person

The gospel of John tells us, "In the beginning was the Word, and the Word was with God, and the Word was God. He was in the beginning with God" (John 1:1-2). A little later the evangelist writes, "And the Word became flesh and He dwelt among us, and we beheld His glory, the glory as of the only begotten of the Father, full of grace and truth" (John 1:14). Jesus truly was Emmanuel, God wrapped in human flesh.

The book of Hebrews opens with these words:

> God, who at various times and in various ways spoke in time past to the fathers by the prophets, has in these last days spoken to us by His Son, whom He has appointed heir of all things, through whom also He made the worlds; who being the brightness of His glory and the express image of His person, and upholding all things by the word of His power, when He had by Himself purged our sins, sat down at the right hand of the Majesty on high (Hebrews 1:1-3).

Although God had revealed something of Himself through the prophets of old, He most completely and perfectly manifested His true nature through His Son, Jesus Christ. This is why Jesus could tell one of His disciples, "Have I been with you so long, and yet have you not known Me, Philip? He who has seen Me has seen the Father" (John 14:9). Earlier He had said, "He who sees Me sees Him who sent Me" (John 12:45). When you observe Jesus, you look into the very soul of God. So the apostle Paul insists that Jesus is the image of the invisible God (Colossians 1:15).

Jesus came to earth to reveal to us what God is really like. As you look at the life of Jesus and study His teachings, you discover His heavenly Father's true nature. Jesus *had* to come, for as John declares,

> No one has seen God at any time. The only begotten Son, who was in the bosom of the Father, He has declared Him [or revealed Him to us] (John 1:18).

Since no one on earth had ever seen God at any time, people had mixed ideas concerning Him and His nature—many of them quite peculiar. And that is why Jesus came, to clear away the misunderstandings and to declare to us the whole truth about God, His heavenly Father.

A Lot of Bad Ideas

Over the centuries, human beings have developed innumerable false ideas and concepts of God. The Greeks believed in many gods who controlled and governed the passions of men. They had a god for each emotion, a deity for each passion. They worshiped the planets, the sun, the moon, and the constellations. They worshiped many gods, all of whom they believed to be selfish and self-centered, interested only in using their powers for their own ends.

The Romans adopted the gods of the Greeks, as well as many other deities from the far-flung lands they conquered. If you go to India today and look at the Hindu temples, you'll get an idea of what it means to worship hundreds and even *millions* of gods—some of whom look horribly grotesque.

So what is God really like?

The Bible says that God committed the revelation of Himself to only one nation, named Israel. So Paul asks in his letter to the Romans,

> What advantage then has the Jew, or what is the profit of circumcision? Much in every way! Chiefly because to them were committed the oracles of God (Romans 3:1-2).

That is, in history God had spoken exclusively to one nation, the Jewish people, and revealed Himself to them.

Moses had said to his countrymen,

> For what great nation is there that has God so near to it, as the Lord our God is to us, for whatever reason we may call upon Him? And what great nation is there that has such statutes and righteous judgments as are in all this law which I set before you this day? (Deuteronomy 4:7-8).

God Himself chose to reveal Himself to this nation. So the psalmist stated,

> He declares His word to Jacob, His statutes and His judgments to Israel. He has not dealt thus with any nation; and as for His judgments, they have not known them (Psalm 147:19-20).

God entrusted ancient Israel with His revelation so that His people might share that revelation with the rest of the world. Unfortunately, they became very clannish and failed to share that revelation of God with the world; instead, they kept it pretty much to themselves. By the time Jesus came to earth, they had so misused God's revelation that Jesus told them,

> Is it not written, "My house shall be called a house of prayer for all nations"? But you have made it a "den of thieves" (Mark 11:17).

He called the religious leaders of the time "blind" and warned they were leading the blind straight into a ditch (Matthew 15:14). He also said, "If your eye is bad, your whole body will be full of darkness. If therefore the light that is in you is darkness, how great is that darkness!" (Matthew 6:23).

In this way, even God's chosen people had developed a false concept of God. They came to believe that God was very exacting and cruel. They thought of Him as harsh, unreasonable, and demanding. They thought God required far more from them than anyone could produce; and so multitudes turned away from God and began to hate His ways—and all because of the exacting, punctilious ways by which they sought to apply their false interpretations of the laws of God.

In such a skewed context, it is easy to see why most people felt they could never draw close to God. They never had a hope of growing intimate with Him—and really, because of their warped concept of God, they didn't especially want to draw close to Him.

Unfortunately, in many places this remains true even to the present day. God still is badly misrepresented. So we see little demigods standing before large crowds and declaring their distorted concepts of God, which are actually just a reflection of themselves and their desire to control their followers. They, too, represent God as demanding and requiring sacrificial support—in truth, only because the leader wants to maintain a lavish lifestyle. And so they make a farce out of God.

Do you see why it was so necessary for Jesus to come and give us a true revelation of God? That little Babe lying in the manger is God incarnate, in human flesh. He would grow up to be a man and would travel around Israel to reveal the truth about the Father. Jesus came for *that* purpose. If you want to know God and understand the truth about God, then you have to look at what Jesus said and did, for in Him you will find the revelation of God.

What Is He Like?

So what kind of things did Jesus say and do to reveal to us the heart of God? Consider Luke 6:27-31:

> Love your enemies, do good to those who hate you. Bless those who curse you, and pray for those who spitefully use you. To him who strikes

> you on the one cheek, offer the other also. And from him who takes away your cloak, do not withhold your tunic either. Give to everyone who asks of you. And from him who takes away your goods do not ask them back. And just as you want men to do to you, you also do to them likewise.

And He wasn't finished! Despite how the people's heads must have been spinning, He then added:

> But love your enemies, do good, and lend, hoping for nothing in return; and your reward will be great, and you will be sons of the Most High. For He is kind to the unthankful and evil. Therefore be merciful, just as your Father is also merciful (Luke 6:35-36).

So then, what major things did Jesus reveal to us about His Father? He revealed that God loves all, even His enemies. Those who make themselves enemies of God—those who oppose God and set their wills against His—He loves despite their rebellion. God does good even to those who hate Him.

Elsewhere Jesus said that God makes the sun to rise on the evil and the good, and He causes rain to fall upon both the just and the unjust (Matthew 5:45). He does good to those who hate Him and He blesses those who curse Him. That's tough; isn't it?

How do we naturally respond if someone curses us? Be honest! And yet, God blesses those who curse Him. Do you remember Jesus' prayer after His enemies had nailed Him to the cross? "Father, forgive them, for they do not know what they do" (Luke 23:34). He *prayed* for those who mistreated Him—and so, in Jesus, we see what God is really like.

God's love is so great that it overcomes all opposition and clears away all obstacles. As the Scripture says, "Or do you despise the riches of His goodness, forbearance, and longsuffering, not knowing that the goodness of God leads you to repentance?" (Romans 2:4). So often it has been the goodness of God that has brought me to my knees. How good He is!

Jesus reminds us of this again when He declares, "Judge not, and you shall not be judged. Condemn not, and you shall not be condemned. Forgive, and you will be forgiven" (Luke 6:37). These are the glorious traits and characteristics of Almighty God. And so John could write, "For God did not send His Son into the world to condemn the world, but that the world through Him might be saved" (John 3:17). Jesus came to forgive us our sins—and He expects His disciples to follow His example and continue to reveal God's loving nature to the world.

Of course, all of these things irritate and oppose our fleshly nature. We don't naturally *like* loving our enemies, doing good to those who hate us, blessing those who curse us, praying for those who mistreat us, turning the other cheek, and refusing to judge or condemn. Jesus knew all about that, and yet He could still say, "Why do you call Me, 'Lord, Lord,' and not do the things which I say?" (Luke 6:46).

On the other hand, why wouldn't we want to do the things that Jesus commands us to do? What do we find so objectionable about them? Don't you think it would be a much better world if everyone followed His commandments and lived by His instructions? Wouldn't *you* like it if everyone treated you as you'd like to be treated?

Imagine if a real estate development somewhere advertised that a new community would sell houses only to loving people, absolutely committed to doing unto others as they would like to have done to them. None of the houses would have locks on the doors. There wouldn't be police departments, judges, courts, nor jails, for all of such issues would be resolved in love and consideration. You wouldn't have to pay people to tell you what you could do and couldn't do—no one telling you that you cannot put up a nativity scene at Christmastime on public property. No one enforcing that you cannot sing Christmas carols in the public schools. No one requiring you to chop down an ugly, old tree in the front of your house. You see, it costs a lot of money to hire people to help control our lives and then to enforce such rules. *That's* why our taxes are so high.

I would be the first to sign up to buy a house in that community. But then I would gladly give up my place in line to someone more needy than I am. I would stand back in consideration and wait my turn until it seemed more convenient for me to sign up—at least, that is what I ought to do.

Media types seem obsessed with portraying how horrible it would be if we lived by Christian principles. "Oh my, Christians might try to impose their value system on everyone. They will teach our children that they shouldn't fight, that they shouldn't cheat, that they shouldn't have sex outside of marriage. And they would probably want to outlaw pornography, adultery, and alcohol. Christians might even impose censorship! That's such a horrible word. They wouldn't allow rap groups to have graphic lyrics and foul language in their songs. Oh, my! We would probably have to spend time with the family. We couldn't hang out at the bars or in the clubs, drinking beer and watching girls dance all night."

Can you imagine how rotten things would be if Christians had their way in society? What a terrible thought!

The Love of God in Christ

Jesus came to this world to show us what God is really like. He especially came to reveal the love of God that made a way for us to live with Him forever in heaven. When people saw Jesus, they saw God's love. And when they gazed upon the cross of Christ, they saw that love poured out to its greatest extent.

"Yes," someone says. "That was great for them two thousand years ago. But Jesus isn't around any longer today. I cannot fly over to Israel and see Him whenever I feel discouraged. How does Jesus coming in the flesh so long ago help me to believe in the love of God today?"

I think a man by the name of Paul can answer that little question.

You see, Paul never saw Jesus "in the flesh," either. He came to faith in Jesus years after the Lord had died, risen from the grave, and ascended into heaven. Yet while he never saw Jesus walking around the villages of Judea or speaking in the temple courts of Jerusalem, he had heard all the apostles' stories about the amazing love of God as displayed in Jesus' life. He had experienced that love for himself through God's Holy Spirit. And he believed so firmly in this divine love—demonstrated by Jesus the Son and rooted in God the Father—that in the eighth chapter of Romans he gave us five of the most precious verses found anywhere in Scripture.

Paul bookends this beautiful passage with divine love. At the beginning he writes of "the love of Christ" and at the end he concludes with "the love of God which is in Christ Jesus our Lord" (Romans 8:35, 39). And in between he makes it clear that *nothing* can ever drive the slightest wedge between God's amazing love and us.

"Who shall separate us from the love of Christ?" Paul asks. "Shall tribulation, or distress, or persecution …" (Romans 8:35). He doesn't mean that we will never have to face those terrible things. Jesus Himself said, "In the world you will have tribulation" (John 16:33). The early church experienced a lot of tribulation. So can that separate you from the love of Christ?

Or how about distress? All of us pass through stressful situations; some of these difficult conflicts can make us feel like giving up. Or what about persecution? That can get pretty bad! Jesus said, "If they persecuted Me, they will also persecute you" (John 15:20). He declared,

> Blessed are you when they revile and persecute you, and say all kinds of evil against you falsely for My sake. Rejoice and be exceedingly glad, for great is your reward in heaven (Matthew 5:11-12).

And James added, "Count it all joy when you fall into various trials" (James 1:2). So can persecution separate you from the love of Christ?

It intrigues me that as I consider the early church, and even as we observe the suffering church today, Satan has never done a good job of destroying the church through persecution. In fact, the church usually becomes stronger and grows under persecution. The devil's most effective weapon is joining the church to bring in compromise, prompting the church to make ungodly concessions in order to gain the world's favor. But can persecution separate you from God's love?

And what about famine or nakedness or peril or sword? What about horrendous natural disasters, homelessness, mortal danger or war? Surely those things have the power to send God's love scurrying away from you! For even Paul says, "As it is written: 'For Your sake we are killed all day long; we are accounted as sheep for the slaughter'" (Romans 8:36). What about that?

As you might expect, Paul has an answer for you: "Yet in all these things we are more than conquerors through Him who loved us" (v. 37).

That's quite a phrase, "more than conquerors." What does it mean to be *more* than a conqueror? We all know what it is to be a conqueror. You go in, you fight the battle, and you win. You are a conqueror. So what is it to be *more* than a conqueror?

That's to go *into* the battle victorious. It is to have the victory even in the midst of battle. While bullets still zip around your head—while the outcome still seems very uncertain—nevertheless, you already have the glorious victory and the glad rejoicing that comes with it. That's what it means to be "more than a conqueror." So as you go into the battle against forces of darkness, against the powers of evil, you go in as a victor. You go in the victory of Jesus Christ. You have already conquered in the middle of the fight. You have victory already in the midst of the conflict. So you can rejoice even in the heat of battle, for you already know the outcome. If God is for you, who can be against you? You know who wins. And thus you are more than a conqueror through Him who loves you.

However, Paul isn't done yet. Not even close! For he goes on,

> For I am persuaded that neither death nor life, nor angels nor principalities nor powers … shall be able to separate us from the love of God (Romans 8:38-39).

Principalities and powers seem to be rankings of angelic beings. In Ephesians 1:20-21, Paul tells how Christ is even now seated in heavenly places, far above *all* "principalities and powers." And in Colossians 2:15, Paul tells us how Jesus, through the cross, triumphed over the "principalities and powers" that opposed us. He even made an open display of His victory. These principalities and powers have no ability to separate you from the love of God in Christ.

"But what about unforeseen things?" someone asks. "What about something that comes totally out of the blue?"

Once again, Paul has an answer for you.

> Nor things present nor things to come, nor height nor depth, nor any other created thing, shall be able to separate us from the love of God which is in Christ Jesus our Lord (Romans 8:38-39).

God's love is simply *inseparable* from you. He will not let you go. He'll hold on to you tight with every ounce of strength in His omnipotent hands. *Nothing* can separate you from His love. Through your faith in Christ, you're His child. He has chosen you. He's called you. He's justified you. He's glorified you, even though you'll still be waiting a little while to see the final result. But it's already done in His mind, and thus, it is an accomplished fact. He has firm control over your life and over all the circumstances of your life. He makes all things work together for good because you love Him and you've been called according to His purposes (see Romans 8:28).

Remember what God said to Jeremiah: "Before I formed you in the womb I knew you; before you were born I sanctified you; I ordained you a prophet to the nations" (Jeremiah 1:5). Even before Jeremiah's conception, God had his life all planned out. He knew him completely before he was even a fertilized egg. And that's true not only of Jeremiah; it's true of you, too! Before you were ever conceived, God knew you. While your body took shape in your mother's womb, God had His plans for your life.

Do you have that kind of confidence in God's love? It's wonderful to know that God is in control, but it's just as important that you yield to God in order that He might fulfill His purposes in and through your life. If that describes you, then you are a happy, peaceful man or woman.

I know that I am totally persuaded of God's love. I'm completely persuaded of His plan. I'm so persuaded of God's overruling, providential care over my life that I do not fear what might happen to me or to anything else. Why not? Because whatever comes, it can come to me only as my loving God allows it to come. God loves me and He'll allow only those things that can work out for my good. He won't allow anything that would destroy me; He permits only those things that will work out for my ultimate good.

Because I have that kind of strong confidence in God, I am persuaded that in all of these things I, too, can be more than a conqueror. God loves me! And He will never allow His love to get separated from me. Not today. Not tomorrow. Not ever.

If you have that kind of confidence in God's love, then you can go through the darkest night and come out the next morning with new life in your heart and a fresh song on your lips. It's all about His love and the confidence that He gives.

The apostle Paul made the case just as airtight as he possibly could. He put in everything he could think of—and yet I know that some poor, timid soul will still stand there and quiver, thinking that God is somehow going to forsake him or her.

"God surely cannot love me anymore. He's through with me! He has had it with me!"

Now, wait a minute. *Nothing* can separate you from the love of God which is in Christ Jesus our Lord. No angel, no principality, no power; nothing that has ever been before or shall ever come after; not things present or things to come; not height or depth or any other created being will *ever* be able to separate you from God's love in Christ. Why not? Because God's love for you is constant. It is eternal. It does not depend on you but upon His own unchanging nature of boundless love. *You* do not cause the slightest bit of God's love for you; therefore, it is constant and it remains. Forever!

God loves you continually, whether you've been good or bad—He loves you for better or for worse, for richer or for poorer, in sickness and in health. He loves you all of the way. His love is there and it is constant. As you face serious problems and battles in life, it's important that you develop a keen awareness and consciousness of God's love actively working on your behalf. God has made available to you His infinite resources. He is there to help, to strengthen, to lift. And if you fall, He's there to pick you up. Never forget that God loves you and is for you.

Satan would have you believe that God is against you because of your failures and weaknesses and bad days. But not so! God delights in you. God knows all about you and yet He takes great delight in you. And nothing—absolutely *nothing, anywhere,* at *any* time, from *any* direction—can separate you from the love of God that is in Christ Jesus your Lord.

Oh, how grateful we should be for the love of God in Christ. May God help us to comprehend the length, the breadth, the depth and the height, and to know the love of Christ that God has for us in Him.

Get Your Reservation In

Every Christmastime, rather than just getting sentimental over a beautiful story about a cute baby born in Bethlehem, stop and think about the purpose of Jesus' coming. He came to show you and me what God is really like. He wanted us to know that God has made a way for us, in love, to spend eternity with Him in heaven through faith in the crucified and risen Son of God, Jesus Christ.

So how would Jesus have you celebrate His coming and His birthday? I think He might have us celebrate by loving our enemies, by doing good to those who hate us—maybe even sending them a Christmas gift this year. For as Jesus said, "If you do good only to those who do good to you—well, big deal. Sinners do that! Or if you love only those who love you, big deal. Tax collectors do that! And if you lend only to those from whom you expect to receive back both principal and interest, that's no big deal. Sinners lend to sinners!" (see Luke 6:32-34).

Jesus calls us to be different. He calls us to do more. Why? Because our Father does more and Jesus came to reveal to us our Father. So if you get caught in a traffic jam today, may the Lord give you the patience you need to make it a pleasant experience for everyone around you. As they honk their horns, feeling all frenzied and harried, you just smile back and blow kisses. In that way you can be a child of your Father who causes His sun to shine upon the just and the unjust.

Incidentally, that community that I told you about? It really does exist. You will never be able to find a better community, because you can never find a better Landlord—a loving, kind, compassionate, gracious, forgiving, helping, strengthening God who seeks to do you good. It's called heaven—and I have my reservation already in.

Do you?

PART TWO

Our Love for God

"We love Him because He first loved us."

1 JOHN 4:19

Your life and mine each has a center point. The big question is: Where does that center point lie? Upon what do our lives revolve? What is the axis upon which our days turn?

Jesus told us that the only way to find purpose and meaning is to orient our lives around God. Why? Because *He is the only center point worth having*. The Lord Almighty must become the center of our existence, the very hub around which the rest of our lives revolve—and that begins to happen for all of us when we willingly and with joy choose to pursue a loving relationship with Him.

Love God supremely! This is the first major step on the road to a life well-led and well worth living.

A New Heart

CAN YOU TELL THE difference between an honest question and a dishonest one? A dishonest question is not looking for an answer; it wants an argument. An honest question, on the other hand, seeks a bona fide answer.

"Since I want to know, I ask a question"—that's honesty.

"Since I have a point to prove, I'll try to get into an argument with you to show you that you're wrong. I ask the question to open the argument"—that's dishonesty.

At this stage in my life, I can tell fairly quickly whether I'm being asked an honest question or a dishonest one. For example, when a person asks me, "Why don't you baptize people the moment they accept Jesus?"

I know I haven't heard an honest question. The person has no real interest in knowing why we don't haul brand new converts down to the beach that night and plunk them under the waves. It's a dishonest question. What they want is a big controversy, because they believe in baptismal regeneration, that a person is not truly saved until they are baptized. And if the new believer should die before next Saturday's baptism he will be lost. So they are all for emergency baptisms—"get 'em into the tank as quickly as possible and dunk 'em."

Since I don't much care for silly controversies over Scripture, the minute I identify a dishonest question, I quit talking. I'm just not interested in getting into a foolish dispute or argument. The Bible says, "If anyone is ignorant, let him be ignorant" (1 Corinthians 14:38). Of course, that verse can apply to me as well as to the next fellow!

Which Is the Greatest?

One day a young man approached Jesus with a question. He had just watched a group of religious leaders ask the Savior a dishonest question and get roasted for it. He, however, had a genuine one: "Which is the first commandment of all?" he wondered.

You could tell this fellow had an honest question burning in his chest. In fact, this question should concern every man or woman who has ever become convinced of the existence of God. The man was asking, "Jesus, what is the most important thing in life?" He didn't try to play a trivia game with Jesus. Nor was he asking about the first commandment God ever gave; that would be the order not to eat of the tree of good and evil in the middle of the garden of Eden. No, he wanted to know about the first commandment *in order of importance*. What was it? Jesus answered him,

> The first of all the commandments is: "Hear, O Israel, the Lord our God, the Lord is one. And you shall love the Lord your God with all your heart, with all your soul, with all your mind, and with all your strength." This is the first commandment (Mark 12:29-30).

Jesus went clear back to Deuteronomy 6:4, to what is known as the *Shema*. This is the portion of Scripture that the Jews used to roll up and wear in little boxes on their wrists or place on their foreheads. On their feast days they would chant it when they gathered in the temple courts. The song would build and build as they called out together, "Hear, O Israel, the Lord our God is one Lord."

When Jesus calls us to love God with all of our heart, all of our soul, all of our mind, and all of our strength, He means that the primary, most important and most basic purpose of our lives is to know and love the true and living God. That's first, above everything else. We are to love and worship *only* the true and the living God—no one else.

And what a love He requires. Jesus says we are to love the one true God with all of our heart (the deepest area of our life), with all of our soul (the conscious area of our life), with all of our mind (the intellectual area of our life—an area that Jesus added to the list), and with all of our strength (the physical area of our life). In other words, He wants us to love God with everything in us, holding nothing back. In fact, we were made for exactly that purpose. God designed us in love that we might love Him in return. It's the whole reason for our existence.

An Alternate Plan

God wanted to make so sure that His people didn't miss this calling that He repeated the same idea in several places and at several times. For example, read what He said through Moses elsewhere:

> And now, Israel, what does the Lord your God require of you, but to fear the Lord your God, to walk in all His ways and to love Him, to serve the Lord your God with all your heart and with all your soul (Deuteronomy 10:12).

So what does God demand? That we reverence Him, that we walk in all of His ways, that we love Him and serve Him with all our heart and all our soul. That's a lot; isn't it? And yet, clearly, we haven't done it. And so you say, "I failed in that. What now?"

The failure of your confession to love God fully doesn't take God by surprise. The Bible says, "For all have sinned and fall short of the glory of God" (Romans 3:23). So does that mean that it's all over; that there's no hope for us? No, thank God! Our loving Lord has an alternate plan.

Some men once came to Jesus with the question, "What shall we do, that we may work the works of God?" (John 6:28). It's the same basic idea: "What does God require of us?" And Jesus replied, "This is the work of God, that you believe in Him whom He sent" (John 6:29).

Praise God, I can do that! Though I failed in the ideal requirement, yet I can fulfill the actual requirement, through faith. What does God require of you and me? That we believe in His Son, Jesus Christ.

You can do that, too. You can handle that. And as you believe in Jesus Christ, you receive a new dynamic for life. Christ comes in and begins to indwell you. By His indwelling power and presence, He begins to give you the strength and the ability to live according to God's divine ideal. He gives you the strength to walk in the ways of righteousness. He gives you the love for God that you lack. He begins to work in you, doing for you what you cannot do for yourself.

God hasn't given up on the divine ideal as proclaimed so long ago through Moses. Rather, through Christ, He is giving you and me the capacity to fulfill that divine ideal. In fact, the moment you believe in Jesus Christ—the instant you commit your life to Him—you fulfill God's requirement.

Don't Choose Frustration

But I suppose I should back up a bit. For although God made us to revolve around His axis, we crash-landed when Adam and Eve disobeyed God in the garden. Ever since then, people naturally choose self-centered lives.

And what's so wrong with that? Well, the Bible assures us that a self-centered life is destined for emptiness and frustration. In fact, the book of Ecclesiastes gives us a classic example of the problem of self-centeredness.

King Solomon lived a wildly self-centered life. He said, "Whatsoever my eyes desired I kept not from them, I withheld not my heart from any joy." He did everything for himself—and ended up with that plaintive cry, "Vanity, vanity," or "Emptiness, emptiness, everything is empty and frustrating!" He did it all and he had it all. But because he centered his entire life around himself and his desires, by the end of his days he found life unfulfilling, disappointing, and eventually ended up as a bitter cynic.

You won't find things any different if *you* live for yourself. When you get to the end of the road you will say, "It wasn't worth it. Life is a mistake, a tragic mistake. It's a farce. There's no meaning nor purpose. I began as an accident and I'll go out as an accident. And there's no reason for my existence."

How empty! How futile! And if you wind up there, it will be because you placed yourself at the center of your life.

The only solution is to place God at the very center of your being. That's what Jesus was getting at in urging us to love God with everything we are. "That's the most important thing," He says. "That's primary. Get God at the center of your life and begin to enjoy a growing, loving relationship with Him."

Have you ever stopped to realize that the first four of the Ten Commandments all deal with your relationship with God? And as Jesus explained, each of those four can be summed up in loving God with all your heart, soul, mind, and strength—that is, giving the Lord your full and complete devotion.

This shouldn't be hard, should it? It sounds like the easiest thing in the world. And it really would be—if only we hadn't all followed Adam and Eve straight into disobedience. The problem is not with God's command; the problem is with our rebellious hearts. And that means if we are ever to find our purpose and fulfill our divine design—and so enjoy God and His universe as He intends—then *something* has to be done about our hard hearts.

Leave it to a loving God to do exactly that!

You Need a New Heart

A fatally serious problem such as a dead, stony heart requires some serious intervention. And just as expected, we discover God had something big in mind from the very beginning. He first mentioned it in the brief, mysterious prophecy of Genesis 3:15, but began to unfold it much more clearly in the time of the prophet Ezekiel.

Ezekiel lived in an age of rampant wickedness, even among his own countrymen. So spiritually dark had the little Hebrew kingdom grown that God announced He was about to destroy the nation through the vicious army of Babylon. There would be no escape, no reprieve. And yet, out of the gloom, a bright ray of hope broke through. Out of His own overflowing love, God promised His people something new:

> I will give them one heart, and I will put a new spirit within them, and take the stony heart out of their flesh, and give them a heart of flesh, that they may walk in My statutes and keep My judgments and do them; and they shall be My people, and I will be their God (Ezekiel 11:19-20).

The hearts of many of us have grown so hard against God that they've become like stone—untouchable, unmovable, without compassion. We have become so set in our sinful ways that we have no intention of changing for anyone. We greet all of God's pleadings and entreaties with stony resistance.

Hearts of stone!

But God said He would exchange those stony hearts for hearts of flesh; soft and pliable hearts that could at last respond to God with all the love and devotion that He had designed for them. Just before Ezekiel began his prophetic ministry, Jeremiah prophesied of the day when God would no longer write His law on tablets of stone, but upon the fleshly tablets of a man's heart. "I will put My law in their minds, and write it on their hearts," God said, "and I will be their God, and they shall be My people" (Jeremiah 31:33-34; Hebrews 8:7-13).

You see what God is really looking for; don't you? He wants a meaningful, loving relationship with you. God doesn't want a legal relationship with you. He has no interest in binding you to Himself through laws. He doesn't want to chain you up. No! He wants a close relationship with you based upon love. He doesn't want some outside law to force you to obey Him; He wants your love for Him to prompt your obedience.

New Desires, Not Old Laws

In the book *Odyssey*, the author Homer illustrated how Odysseus left his home to fight in the Trojan War, despite great reluctance. After the war had ended, it took Odysseus twelve long years to return home.

At some point Odysseus and his fellow sailors would have to cruise past a magical island inhabited by half nymph/half women called sirens. These creatures sang so beautifully—and yet so murderously—that their songs enchanted all men who dared to sail past their island. The enchanted sailors would inevitably drive their ships into the rocky shore, killing everyone on board. The sirens prided themselves on the fact that no mortal had ever shown the strength to resist their song.

Since Odysseus wanted to hear that gorgeous melody, he directed his men to put wax in their ears and then to chain him up to the mast of the ship—his own ears wide open. As his ship sailed past the enchanted island, Odysseus heard the impossibly beautiful music of the sirens. He begged his men to turn the ship toward the shore. He screamed, he threatened, he railed, he cursed. He nearly went mad. But the wax in their ears prevented them from hearing not only the sirens, but also his lunatic commands. And so they sailed on. Odysseus survived, but nearly lost his mind.

Ancient mythology also tells another story about the sirens, this time about a gifted musician named Orpheus. This man and his crew also sailed by the island of the sirens. As their bewitching music wafted over the waves, the enchanted sailors began to turn their ship toward shore. Once Orpheus woke up and grasped their peril, he immediately took out his flute and began to play music so far superior to that of the sirens that his men lost all interest in the enchanted song. And so they rowed safely by.

We all know religious people who, like Odysseus, feel chained to the Lord. They long for the songs of this world. So they struggle and whine and wish with everything in them that they could just cut loose and plunge into the dark world of the sirens. "These laws have chained me to God." they complain.

That's a miserable place to be; I don't recommend it to anybody. When your heart longs for the things of the world, but you feel chained to righteous principles, then you're stuck in a legal relationship with God. And you feel utterly downcast.

How much better to hear the infinitely more beautiful song of the Lord! How delightful to feel so attracted by His love and His beauty that the world loses its appeal. Once you have genuinely gazed upon His splendor and experienced His glory, then the call of the siren loses its allure. A desire for the things of this world no longer has a hold upon you. You gladly turn your ears to the beautiful music of the Lord, at the same time turning away from those who would lure you to your death.

This is exactly what God said He was going to do in the hearts of His people. He promised to give them a new heart, a heart of flesh. He would take away the stony heart so that they could enjoy a loving relationship with Him. Their new heart of flesh would *desire* to keep His statutes and *want* to keep His ordinances.

God will never force you to serve Him or to love Him. But if you will ask Him, He will change your heart and give you a new longing for the things of the Spirit.

A Beautiful Thing to Watch

I've observed with keen interest how God changes the heart and attitude of a person who accepts Jesus Christ as Savior. As the Bible says, "Therefore, if anyone is in Christ, he is a new creation; old things have passed away; behold, all things have become new" (2 Corinthians 5:17).

I've seen some of the hardest characters imaginable—people with tough, bitter hearts—become tender and even affectionate once they accept Jesus Christ as Savior. It's a beautiful thing to observe.

Decades ago when we lived in Tucson, we had some marvelous next-door neighbors named Jim and Jan. Jan was the first to receive the Lord. God's Spirit started working in her heart in a marvelous way and she had a terrific conversion. What a thrilling moment when she accepted Christ! She had a very bubbly kind of personality and the Lord just enhanced her whole identity.

Immediately Jan wanted to tell her husband that she had accepted the Lord. But he was a hard man, especially against the things of the Lord. So she felt she ought to wait for a more appropriate time to tell her story of conversion.

That evening when Jim came home from work, however, their youngest daughter started jumping up and down with great excitement. "Mama," she said breathlessly, "are you going to tell Daddy what happened when Chuck came over today?" She kept it up until Jim finally said, "What in the world goes on when I'm not at home?"

So Jan told her husband how she had received Jesus Christ. She described how she had instantaneously felt a wave of peace and joy flood her spirit. She didn't completely realize it yet, but this is the work of God's Spirit—giving a new heart.

At first, Jim reacted very negatively. But some time later when we began to talk about it, I had the privilege of kneeling down with him as he, too, accepted the Lord. Shortly afterwards he and Jan got transferred to Alaska. And just a few days later I received a letter from Jim that I will cherish forever. In it he thanked me for sharing Jesus with him and for introducing him to a brand new life in Christ.

"Chuck," he wrote, "it used to be that I hated children, even though I had three beautiful daughters. I said children were the scourge of the earth. I felt trapped in my marriage and with my children—but I cannot describe how God has changed my heart."

Jim had to leave for Alaska before the rest of his family could join him, and he wrote the letter to me before his loved ones had arrived at their new home. "I'm up here finding myself missing them desperately," he wrote. "I cannot wait for them to get here so I can embrace them and have them with me." And then he added the clincher: "I cannot understand myself—but I'm such a different person."

That's *exactly* what God said He was going to do! He promised to take out the stony heart and replace it with a heart of flesh. Remarkable changes would come from within, not from some outward and oppressive kind of legal bondage.

God doesn't *want* to sign you up for some lifeless contract. Unlike what many people think, He doesn't "play the game." Whenever you miss some detail, He doesn't say, "C'mon, Bud, you didn't read the fine print!" He has no desire to keep you in a binding, legal arrangement. He's interested in a loving relationship with you. That's why He wants to give you a new heart, a heart that truly loves God and the things of God.

How Can It Happen?

I realize that if you don't yet have this "new heart," you probably don't quite understand what I'm talking about. It sounds as though I'm speaking mysteries. How can a man be changed? Can a leopard change his spots? How can a man have a whole new life when he is old? How can these things be?

A man named Nicodemus had these very questions for Jesus. The Master spoke to him of new life, of new birth, of a new dimension of life after the Spirit—and Nicodemus simply didn't understand. "How can this be?" he wondered. "How can a man be born again when he is old? He cannot return to his mother's womb to be born a second time; can he?" (John 3:1-21).

Jesus replied, "That which is born of the flesh is flesh; but that which is born of the Spirit is spirit." In other words, "It all has to start with God, Nicodemus; that's why My Father promised to give His people a new heart and a new spirit. Where else could they obtain such a heart of flesh?"

But *how* could such a remarkable transformation take place? John explains in the most famous verse of the Bible: "For God so loved the world that He gave His only begotten Son, that whoever believes in Him should not perish but have everlasting life" (John 3:16). When you believe in Jesus Christ—when you choose to ask Him to come into your life and to change you—God gives you that new heart and new spirit.

I don't understand the ways of the Spirit, but I do know He works to put a new spirit within you. He gives you a new heart of flesh. And at that moment, your life is transformed. You're changed forever. The things you once hated, you now begin to love. And the things you once loved—the activities and attitudes that felt so important to you—you begin to abhor. Why? Because now you see them for what they really are: instruments of destruction.

It doesn't matter how hard your heart may have been or how bitter you have felt against the Lord. The Holy Spirit of God can change all of that in a moment's time. Years of bitterness can be removed in an instant when Jesus comes into your life.

Where Is Your Heart?

Where is your heart today? Jeremiah said, "The heart is deceitful above all things, and desperately wicked; who can know it?" (Jeremiah 17:9).

God responded to the prophet's question like this: "I, the Lord, search the heart, I test the mind, even to give every man according to his ways, according to the fruit of his doings" (v. 10). He means that He searches your heart in order to know it thoroughly. And when God judges, He will base His judgment on the deepest issues of your heart.

So then, when God says you are to love Him alone with everything within you, how does your own heart stack up? In the secret recesses of your heart, do other gods sit enthroned? Do other issues take precedence over your relationship with God? Do you consider some things more important than the things of the Lord?

Paul told the Romans, "Look, just because you are doing the expected religious things—just because you observe the Sabbath, just because you read the law, just because you've been circumcised—does not make you a child of God. God looks at your heart. It is what's in your heart that counts" (Romans 2:17-29).

In the same way, just because you attend church, sing spiritual songs, and know the Bible well enough to say, "Amen, preach it, brother!" doesn't mean that you are a child of God. You can be baptized, pray, tithe, preach, and do all sorts of other religious things and still not have a right relationship with God. He looks at your heart. That's what counts.

The ancient Jews had a very interesting way of expressing grief or sorrow when some great calamity overtook them. They would rip their clothes—just shred them. When bad news came, they'd say, "Oh, no," and rrrrrrrip. It was their way of expressing their deep feelings of sorrow, grief, or remorse.

Through the prophet Joel, God said to them, "I want you to tear your heart, not your garments. Let your heart be ripped! I want a change there. This outward display of torn clothing, that doesn't count for much. What matters is what's going on in the heart. That's what really interests Me" (Joel 2:13).

Don't deceive yourself. God already knows what is in your heart. The Father says to you, "I know what's in your heart. You don't deceive Me. You might be deceiving yourself, but you will never mislead Me."

If you will just allow Him, God will search your heart and lead you into His path. He will show you, if you're really interested, what is in your heart. It might shock you. It might surprise you—but you need to know the real condition of your heart.

If you have not already done so, I urge you to surrender your heart to God today. Ask the Father to give you a clean heart, a pure heart, a heart of flesh as promised in Ezekiel 11:19-20. Only then will you be able to love Him with all of your heart.

Rocks into Hearts

The first time you travel to Jerusalem, get prepared to see *a lot* of rocks. Many first-time visitors feel overwhelmed by the number of rocks scattered around the city. It's easy to see why the ancients practiced stoning for capital crimes. I've never seen so many rocks in one place. You also might hear quite a few stories about how these rocks got there. One says that God commissioned two angels to scatter rocks across the globe. One angel flew all over the world, scattering the rocks, but the other was lazy. He just dumped them all on Jerusalem.

My favorite story is the one I heard from our tour guide in Israel. He said that God has placed in the heart of every individual a desire to see Jerusalem. Through the years, as time goes by, a person begins to worry that this desire may never be fulfilled. The person's heart begins to grow heavy as that old desire to see Jerusalem remains unfulfilled. It grows heavier and heavier until it becomes like a stone.

But one glorious day, God gives the individual an opportunity to visit Jerusalem. As he approaches the city of God, he feels such joy and elation that he takes that old heart of stone and casts it aside. At last his dream has come true! Before him, with his own eyes, he drinks in the holy city of God.

So all those rocks you see piled around Jerusalem are actually the stony hearts of countless visitors.

Many of us have stony hearts made hard and bitter through difficult experiences, bitter disappointments, and terrible injustices. Our hearts grow hard against the Lord until they become like a stone.

The good news of Jesus Christ is that God can take those hearts of stone and replace them with hearts of flesh—sensitive, tender, loving. He can melt all the bitterness and take away all the hardness and leave behind a beautiful work of His Spirit. That is the only way to love God with all your heart and soul and mind and strength. And it is the only way to discover and to enjoy God's loving purpose for you.

An Undivided Heart

THE POPULAR SONGS FROM my younger days really date me. One song used to ask, "Is you is or is you ain't my baby? The way you're actin' lately makes me doubt."[3] I wonder if God doesn't sometimes feel like singing similar lines to us? "Is you is, or is you ain't My baby? Because the way you're actin' lately makes Me doubt."

Another old song declared, "All, or nothing at all." The songwriter meant, "I want all of your love, or none of it. And if I cannot have it all, I would rather have nothing at all." And I think, *surely the Lord is pleading with us today to love Him with a whole and undivided heart.*

---

3 *Is You Is or Is You Ain't My Baby*, words and music by Billy Austin and Louis Jordan, 1944.

Or I think of yet another fellow described in an old song who had one foot in the rowboat and one foot on the dock—just trying to hedge his bets. Too often, I fear, we put part of our trust in Jesus and part in our Wall Street stock—and so our hearts are divided.

I'd go so far as to say that one of the greatest problems today is a double heart. With part of our heart, we want to serve the Lord; and with another part of our heart, we want to follow after the flesh. I know that pull, and I'm pretty sure you do, too.

The Idols Live On

So many things of this world attract us. I'm personally attracted by intellectualism. I have a strong desire to spend my time studying and learning.

Some individuals have so given themselves over to the development of their intellectual prowess that they spend every moment learning, seeking knowledge, and working to pile up facts. It becomes an obsession. It takes over their daily lives until they spend all their time searching and learning. The Bible describes them as "always learning and never able to come to the knowledge of the truth" (2 Timothy 3:7). As I said, I find this a very attractive allurement for myself.

Others feel more attracted by pleasure. They live for excitement, a thrill, a rush, a wild sensation. They orient their whole lives around moments of exhilaration. Maybe it's that last-minute field goal or a ninth-inning homerun. Many people feel obsessed with pleasure and will spend any amount of money in order to experience that one special, fleeting moment of thrill.

Still others feel attracted by power. They want to control others, to make them grovel at their feet. They want people to beg them for their favor. And so they run for city council, and then state assembly, then state senate, then for the governor's office, and then finally for the Presidency. All the while they're thinking, *What will the people say?*

How will they respond? Will they vote for me in the next election? And so they spend an entire lifetime absorbed in developing ever-greater positions of power.

In ancient times people lived much closer to nature and so also usually lived closer to reality. Living as we do in this crazy, mixed-up culture, we can become very detached from real life. We've become so sophisticated and so chic that it is easy for us to lose touch with reality.

Long ago, people who worshiped pleasure recognized pleasure as their god, and so they carved out a little image and said, "This is Molech. He is the god of pleasure, the god of thrills and excitement." And so they sat little Molech in their homes and burned incense before him. They lit candles around him and prayed: "Let the surf be up!"

What were they doing? They were acknowledging Molech as the god of their life. They were saying, "I live for pleasure. This is more important to me than anything else." The only thing they did that we fail to do is to give their desire a physical shape—they made a wooden or stone idol out of it.

Those who worshiped power carved a different little idol. They called this god Mammon and put him in their homes, built him altars, and offered him their worship. They came and knelt before him and prayed for power over others. Since they recognized they had deified their obsession for power, they were honest about it and said, "I worship power, represented by this little idol."

Men and women obsessed with intellectual pursuits recognized knowledge as their lord, so they called their god Baal (Baal means "lord"). They made their own little idol, bowed down to him, prayed to him, and burned incense as an acknowledgment of their chief goal in life: to gain knowledge.

Back in Bible days, when God spoke to all these folks about their idol worship, they knew exactly what He was talking about. Today, however, when we read Bible verses about idolatry, we tend to get very smug. "I don't have any idols," we say. "I can take you to the family room or the entryway and you won't see any little god sitting on the table." And so we proclaim, quite self-righteously that we don't worship idols—when in reality, we *do* worship the very same principles that ancient people once personified with little wood or stone gods. Like them, we also prioritize our whole lives around learning, around pleasure, around power, or around some other obsessive desire.

A Problem Made Worse

Idols never satisfy anyone, of course, but for Christians, the problem gets much worse. A believer may have a heart to serve the Lord and want to be counted among God's servants. But he also has a heart for the trinkets of the world, and in practice he often gets caught up in worldly activities.

He has given a place in his heart to the Lord, but he hasn't given his *whole* heart to Him. He feels drawn by the Spirit after the things of God, but he also feels drawn by his flesh after the things of the world.

While you'll usually find him in church on Sunday, the rest of the week God has very little place in his life. He seldom communicates with God. He gets so busy in the activities of daily life that God gets squeezed out. And thus, his heart is divided. He feels drawn toward God and the things of the Spirit, but also drawn toward the world.

So often we can feel so pulled by the attractions of the world that our devotion to God becomes something less than total. Do you ever struggle with this? I confess that I sometimes do. And as I feel drawn by this attraction and pulled by this desire, my heart is divided.

The Misery of a Divided Heart

I've never known someone with a badly divided heart (including me) who didn't feel miserable. It's terrible to see.

Such a person has enough of the Lord in his heart to feel very uncomfortable in ungodly surroundings—so he cannot enter fully into the "fun." He has a check in his spirit that keeps him from plunging totally into the world.

And yet he has too much of the world in his heart to be fully happy in Jesus, to have real joy in the Lord. He has a hook in his soul attached to the world by a long chain, which keeps him from fully giving his life to Jesus.

And so he's miserable.

Such a person finds himself in a constant state of turmoil. Practically every moment of every day, he feels continually pulled in two directions. On one side he feels tugged by his desire for Jesus, while on the other side he senses a strong attraction for the things of the world. Usually he winds up with a very strong approach-avoidance conflict, which can create serious neurosis.

Misery—it's just one result of a divided heart.

The Many Troubles of a Divided Heart

A divided heart will do more than make you miserable. It will make your life difficult and cause an endless stream of problems for you. Think about this from the other side for a moment. What do you know about people with divided hearts? I can think of at least three major weaknesses they all have.

1. A divided heart often will not stick around.

People with divided hearts do not make good allies or even good friends. In a time of crisis, such men and women are apt to break ranks and run. You simply cannot rely on them.

Imagine you are a woman looking for a husband. You certainly don't want some fellow with a divided heart. He's likely to say, "Oh yes, I love you—as well as every other little doll on the block." No way! You want his heart to be single toward you. You cannot afford to constantly question his devotion.

The same is true for a fellow looking for a bride. He wants someone with singleness of heart toward him, one in whom he can trust, one who will not flirt with every guy who comes along. No one wants a divided heart in a trusted companion, friend, or spouse.

First Chronicles 12:33 describes how fifty thousand men of Zebulun once gathered before David to present themselves as loyal soldiers. These experts in war would not break rank. In the heat of battle, when the pressure was on, David could count on these men to stand together. The *King James Version* of the Bible declares, "They were not of double heart." And it also says "they came to Hebron with a loyal heart, to make David king over all Israel" (v. 38).

True strength never lies in numbers. It doesn't lie even in abilities. True strength always lies in singleness of heart.

2. A divided heart is not committed to winning.

The half-hearted person can never be a consistent winner. He may gather a few victories along the way, but almost always by accident.

No coach is apt to choose players with half-hearted attitudes toward winning. He won't select guys who come prancing onto the field saying, "My, what a beautiful day! What lovely flowers! I suppose we should practice. Isn't it nice that it doesn't matter whether we win or lose?" Any decent coach would say, "Get out of here!" He wants his players completely devoted to winning. He wants victory to be an obsession with them. That's why you may hear him quote the old saying, "Winning isn't everything—it's the only thing." He wants his team completely into the game. He certainly doesn't want any divided hearts.

The Bible says that a double-minded man is unstable in all of his ways (James 1:8). In other words, you cannot trust him. When things get tough, when the chips are down, he may just give up since it doesn't matter much to him whether you win or lose. "Hey, if it gets rough, I'll just walk away. I'm not committed to this thing." True commitment never lies in words or intentions. True commitment always lies in singleness of heart.

3. A divided heart is unsure of who he or she is.

People with divided hearts do not have a clear idea of where they stand with the Lord. Therefore, whenever it feels convenient and advantageous, they can put on the Christian shield and sing the choruses of the church. If they're with the other crowd, of course, they can look just like anybody else in that group. They're spiritual chameleons suffering from a divided heart.

Much worse, however, when dark days come, they don't know how best to ask the Lord for His help. They don't know Him well. They don't know His Word. They don't remember His promises. They may hope they have eternal life, but they wouldn't put too big of a bet on it. So they grow fearful, anxious, and discouraged—and at that moment, all the chameleon skin in the world doesn't bring them an ounce of comfort.

True confidence will never lie in fitting in and it doesn't lie in adaptability. Faith and true confidence will always lie in singleness of heart.

A Divided Heart Is Lukewarm

A divided heart is a nauseating, lukewarm condition. Lukewarm water occurs when you turn on both hot and cold taps. It's a mixture of the two.

Jesus doesn't think much of it, especially in your relationship with Him.

The Lord once told the ancient church of Laodicea that it had grown lukewarm—and He didn't mean it as a compliment. "I know your works, that you are neither cold nor hot," He said to them. "I could wish you were cold or hot. So then, because you are lukewarm, and neither cold nor hot, I will vomit you out of My mouth" (Revelation 3:15-16).

The Lord cannot tolerate a lukewarm spiritual condition. He doesn't want a divided heart. He doesn't ask to be just a part of your life. He doesn't want you to include Him among the other gods you worship. He desires that you give Him your whole heart, soul, mind, and body—everything.

Jesus has zero interest in a lukewarm relationship with you; in fact, it's nauseating to Him. He wants your heart. He wants your undivided devotion, not some double-hearted fondness. He wants nothing but singleness of heart from you.

You may try to split your devotion between God and something or someone else, but it cannot be done. Jesus said, "No one can serve two masters; for either he will hate the one and love the other, or else he will be loyal to the one and despise the other. You cannot serve God and mammon" (Matthew 6:24).

And yet how many people seek to do just that? They attempt to serve both God and mammon.

Jesus insists, however, that you cannot ride the fence forever. You cannot maintain divided loyalties. You cannot live after the Spirit and walk after the flesh at the same time. It simply won't work. These things are mutually exclusive. You have to choose one or the other.

So don't try juggling God and mammon. Don't attempt to offer lukewarm water to Jesus. The ancient Israelites did, and they wished they hadn't.

It's a Big Deal

We have to realize how much God detests a divided heart. When ancient Israel became spiritually lukewarm toward God, the Lord didn't sit idly by. He said, "Their heart is divided; now they are held guilty." And how did He respond? "He will break down their altars; He will ruin their sacred pillars" (Hosea 10:2).

Had George Gallup lived in that era and conducted a poll, he probably would have discovered that 95 percent of the people believed in the existence of God; 87 percent of them attended a worship service sometime during the year; 92 percent of them felt religion was important in a person's life; and 90 percent believed they should have prayer in the public schools.

Yet almost 100 percent of the people of Hosea's era had a divided heart. Despite a general belief in God, their hearts had become divided, disloyal, and lukewarm toward God. This had occurred even though God had greatly blessed Israel and it had become a very prosperous nation. Sadly, the people used their prosperity to make ornate altars to other gods. They used the goodness of the land, which God had given them, to create and worship dead idols. God kept giving, but nothing came back to Him. In fact, the more God gave, the more they turned to other gods.

The Israelites used their surplus funds to buy large screen TVs, season tickets for Red Sox games, and a condo in Aspen. No, the Bible doesn't really say that; but had they lived today, the text might well have said exactly such a thing. They simply offered their sacrifices to the puny, worthless things that had captured their hearts.

So they made images to Molech, the god of pleasure—and thereby acknowledged that pleasure had mastered their lives. They made images of Ashtoreth, thereby acknowledging that their sexual desires had grown paramount. At least they were honest about it! By their actions they said, "Yes, these are our top priorities. They rule our lives."

And they continued to go to synagogue every Sabbath, where they read from the Torah and said a few prayers. Then for the rest of the week they pursued their own pleasures and desires. They had divided hearts.

Oh, God did have a place in their hearts—but only a very small place. They spent most of their energy on other gods. They became like the foreigners transplanted to Israel by the Assyrians: "So they feared the Lord, yet served their own gods" (2 Kings 17:33). God forbid that the Super Bowl should come on a Sabbath, for then they would have to miss synagogue!

What did God do about the divided hearts and lukewarm attitudes of His people? He promised to break down their altars and spoil their images. It's as though He said, "These things of the world that you have given your heart to—these trinkets that have taken your heart away from Me, these possessions that you have striven to acquire—I will strip them all from you. I am about to take away your altars and destroy your images. They have attracted you away from Me and created your divided hearts, so I will utterly destroy them."

Look at the world around you. Observe all the material things you find so attractive—and realize that they're all going to burn. God will destroy them all. Only one kind of treasure is eternal, the spiritual treasure you lay up in heaven. The rest is wood, hay, and stubble (1 Corinthians 3:11-15). It's all going to burn.

God reserves the non-flammable stuff for those with undivided hearts.

How Is Your Heart?

If you were to write a letter to God, how would you sign it? "All my love, Chuck," "Devotedly yours, Charles." Remember that although you may be able to fool people with words, you can never use them to fool God. And though you might sign, "Devotedly yours," God looks at the things to which you have *really* been devoting yourself—and you cannot fool Him.

First John 3:18 says, "Let us not love in word or in tongue." Words are cheap; anybody can utter them. But we are to love with deeds and in truth. Your actions show where your devotion truly lies, and God wants your undivided devotion. He wants you to give your time and your heart wholly to Him.

So take an honest look at your own heart. Would you classify it as united or divided?

"Well, I serve God," you say. "I go to church." Good! But is there any division there? Think back over this past week. To what did you devote yourself? What activities took up most of your time?

"I devoted a lot of time to my garden," someone says. "I devoted a lot of time to the beach," somebody else says. To what did you devote your time? It can be quite an eye-opener to look around and see what is absorbing your energies, your time, and your mind. The truth is, those are the things to which you are devoted.

Attending church week after week is no guarantee of singleness of heart. Even as you sit there, your mind can roam. You may be in the house of the Lord on Sunday morning, but thinking about going to some bar that night. You may spend Sunday in church, but have no other contact with God the rest of the week.

That's a divided heart.

Again, make an honest personal inventory of yourself. Would you describe your relationship with the Lord as hot? Are you fervently following Jesus Christ? Is He truly the Lord and Master of your life? Is He first and foremost? Is He above everything else? Do you esteem Him above everything else? Or do you have more of a casual relationship with Jesus—it's nice, but you could easily do without it?

If you cannot say, "Yes, I have a fervent relationship with the Lord. He is everything to me." then most likely you have a divided heart. You're lukewarm. And God is calling you to make a change.

What Can I Do?

God will not tolerate a divided heart. He doesn't want half of your devotion or part of your loyalty. He wants you to worship and serve Him alone, with your whole heart.

So what can you do about a divided heart? What is the cure? All of us feel the pull and the pressure of the world. What can we do?

After Jesus commended the church of Ephesus for all of its marvelous activities and works, He said, "Nevertheless I have this against you, that you have left your first love" (Revelation 2:4). The Savior accused them of a divided heart. Somehow they had drifted away from their former burning love of God.

Drifting from God is a slow, nearly imperceptible process of floating along on the waves until we find ourselves adrift without moorings. We're far out at sea and we don't know how we got there. Jesus told the Ephesians, "You've left your first love"—but then He gave them the remedy, a cure with three parts.

First, He said, "Remember therefore from where you have fallen" (v. 5). Can you remember those days when you first discovered the glorious love of God in Jesus Christ? Recall the delightful time when you realized the grace of God had washed you and cleansed you of all of your sins. You felt so excited and so thrilled about the Lord. You were so in love with Him when you realized how much He loved you. You just couldn't get enough! Every time the church doors opened, you were there with your Bible, hungering after God and thirsting after the things of the Spirit. And oh, how your life bubbled over with joy and excitement as you walked with Jesus in close fellowship!

Secondly, Jesus says simply, "Repent" (v. 5). That is, turn around! You've drifted so far away that now you're way out to sea. Turn again! Ask God to forgive you for the coldness you've allowed to come into your relationship. Don't let things stay as they are. Repent!

And finally Jesus advised them, "Repeat." That is, "do the first works" (v. 5). He says to the Ephesians, and to you, to do your first works over again. Go back to the things you were doing when you were so in love with Him. Maybe it was regular Bible study. Maybe it was evangelism. Maybe it was helping out at the local rescue mission. Whatever it was, repeat what you once did.

Remember. Repent. Repeat.

Long before Jesus gave this potent prescription, King David had to find some way to cure his own wandering heart. His remedy began with prayer. We find the heart of his prayer in the simple petition, "Unite my heart to fear Your name" (Psalm 86:11).

David realized this world offered a lot of attractive things that drew his heart after them, things that would divide his heart and prevent him from serving God with his whole heart. So he prayed for God to unite his heart in love for his Lord. In other words, "God, give me singleness of heart toward You. Do not let me come to a place of deception, where I think all I have to do is attend church on Sunday morning and everything will be okay. Give me a heart united toward You."

Like David, you can ask God to unite your heart to serve Him. Pray, "God, just take away this divided heart. I know I cannot serve two masters. I know I'm being divided; I'm being pulled. Give me a united heart, that I might love and serve You."

When you faithfully follow these prescriptions, you will enjoy the same marvelous recovery that David did. God answered his prayer and granted him a renewed relationship with the Lord. And so David exulted, "I will praise You, O Lord my God, with all my heart, and I will glorify Your name forevermore" (Psalm 86:12).

When God unites your heart, then you too will praise Him with *all* of your heart. Once more your heart will overflow with love for God and you will gladly serve Him with everything within you. God yearns for that kind of undivided love from us.

So let us say, "Renew the fire within our hearts, O Lord. Give us once more a burning passion for You."

The Power of a United Heart

Back when I was in high school, we used to listen to a popular song that had a lot in common with the psalms of lament. This poor young man talked on and on about his girlfriend, who was neither too hot nor too cold, neither too meek nor too bold. She just didn't express strong emotions for her boyfriend one way or another.

Finally he said, "And baby, you got to be this or that. You cannot be on the fence. You got to be on one side or the other."

That's just how it is in our relationship with the Lord. We cannot sit on the fence. We have to be this or that. God wants to see our hearts totally toward Him, single toward Him—white-hot.

Jesus took eleven men who had one heart to make Him King, and with those eleven men He turned the world upside down. Those eleven men altered the history of humankind more profoundly than any other group. Why?

Because they had one heart to proclaim Jesus Christ as King.

Oh, may God remove from us the double heart. May He unite our hearts to make Jesus Christ King in order that we might be strong and that we too might have a profound effect upon our own world.

A Heart That Loves Him Supremely

SEVERAL YEARS AGO A fellow came up to me at church and said, "Chuck, I want you to have a new car."

I laughed.

"I never buy a new car," I replied. "Too much depreciation. I let someone else take the loss."

He didn't give up. "I own a dealership here in Orange County," he said, "and I want you to come over and pick out the car you want. I'm going to take the depreciation off the price. I'll give it to you at my cost and you can pick all the options you want; I'll even put them on."

So I went to the dealership and picked out my dream car—all the options General Motors offered, and the color I wanted. He sent the order into Detroit and GM built the car. Soon he called me to say, "Your car is here."

Immediately I went over to pick it up. I turned in my old, used car and drove out of the dealership with a beautiful, brand new convertible. I'd never owned a new car—and the fragrance was all mine. That special new car smell belonged to *me!*

As I drove out of the dealership, I just knew that everybody was watching me. It felt like people's heads turned to look as I passed by in my fancy new car. Oh man, it was nice to drive. All the way home I kept praising the Lord and worshiping Him.

"Lord, You're so good! Wow! This is outrageous! I love it! You are so good to me, Lord. I love You!"

Before I had left for the dealership my wife had asked me to pick up some milk on my way home, so I stopped at a grocery store. As I walked down the aisles, I kept praising the Lord. I just knew everyone in the parking lot had to be admiring my new baby. Man, I was so enamored by it.

"Oh Lord, You're so good. I love You so much! Lord, this is glorious!"

I paid for the items and almost skipped back to my new honey—and there I saw that some inconsiderate nincompoop had carelessly and recklessly put a *ding* in the driver's side door of my dream car!

AND I HADN'T EVEN GOTTEN HER HOME YET!

Enraged and determined to get even, I set to work trying to recover some tiny paint scraping. I hoped to play detective and determine the color of the assault vehicle. *Maybe it's still here in the parking lot and I can pound on somebody!*

All the way home from the store, I fussed and stewed. I felt miserable, absolutely miserable. *Rotten people, rotten world! I hate people, I just hate them. Inconsiderate louts!* Boy, you can be glad I'm not God. I would have sent half the world to hell in the last second!

At home, as I yanked the groceries into the house, my son, Chuck Junior, said to me, "Hey, Dad. Did you get your new car?"

"Yeah," I grumbled.

"Oh, I want to see it!" he exclaimed.

"Sure," I grunted. So I took him out to the car, where he put the top up and down and did all the push-button things—windows, seats, the whole nine yards. Then, as he stood back to admire her, he paused and asked, "Oh, Dad—what's *that*?"

My nose flared as I said, "Would you *believe* that while I was in the market, some stupid, dirty, rotten ..." and I started to launch into my whole little tirade again.

Chuck cocked his head at me slightly and said, "Hey, Dad—it's all going to burn."

Whatever I had intended to say next died in my throat. What could I say? He was absolutely right. "Thank you, son," I replied quietly. "I needed that."

How quickly I had lost perspective! The shininess of the new car, its luxury appointments, the admiring looks I'd received—I had allowed these things to take my focus off of the only truly priceless treasure in the universe. I had gone from "I love You, Lord!" to "I hate the worthless people You created!" in about .003 seconds.

How easy it is to say, "I love You, Lord!" as you're styling down the street in your hot new set of wheels. Ah, but loving Him supremely, *whatever* comes? I find that I still have a ways to go on that one.

The Prostitute and the Pharisee

Did you know that Jesus never turned down an invitation to dinner? It's true. Every time in the Gospels when someone asked Jesus to dinner, He accepted.

Jesus loved eating with people. In fact, sometimes He even invited Himself. During a visit to Jericho, for example, a short man named Zacchaeus climbed a tree to get a glimpse of Jesus. The Lord stopped right beneath him and said, "Hey Zacchaeus! Come on down, because I'm on my way over to your place for dinner" (Luke 19:1-10).

Even in the last book of the Bible, Jesus closes out His messages to the seven churches by saying, "Behold, I stand at the door and knock. If anyone hears My voice and opens the door, I will come in to him and dine with him" (Revelation 3:20). Why does the Lord so love eating with people? It's because He loves the close kind of intimacy that happens only when people share a meal together.

One day a Pharisee named Simon asked Jesus to come for dinner. While we don't know the reason for his invitation, we do know Simon was a rather ungracious host. In those days, since people wore open sandals on dusty roads, most hosts would have a servant waiting at the door with a basin of fresh water to wash each guest's feet. If you could not afford a servant, at least you provided some water. Simon didn't even offer that.

As guests entered the house, the host would lay his hand upon his friend's shoulder and give him the kiss of peace, often touching both cheeks. It was considered common courtesy. Simon did not do that either.

Next, the host would put a drop of rose perfume upon the head of each guest. This gesture lent a lovely fragrance to the atmosphere and said in a practical way, "Let's have a beautiful time together." Nor did Simon do that.

Most houses of that era were built around a courtyard, a good place for feasts. Guests sat on the floor around a low table, leaning on their left elbows with their feet behind them. As they reclined, they used their right hand to eat.

Whenever someone invited a rabbi to dinner, they always left the door open for the public to come in. Uninvited guests could stand around the outer circle and listen to the rabbi.

On that particular day, a streetwalker came to the dinner uninvited. The Greek term used to describe her identifies her as a prostitute; that's how she made her living. She came and stood behind the Master to listen to Him speak.

As she stood there, Jesus' very presence did something in her heart. She became very conscious of her sin and she began to weep, sobbing over her sinful state. As her tears began to fall near the feet of Jesus, she knelt down and began to wipe His feet dry with her hair. And then she began to kiss Jesus' feet and dab them with some perfume she had carried with her in a little alabaster box. Luke describes what happened next:

> Now when the Pharisee who had invited Him saw this, he spoke to himself, saying, "This Man, if He were a prophet, would know who and what manner of woman this is who is touching Him, for she is a sinner" (Luke 7:39).

You should understand that the Pharisees were *very* careful not to touch "sinners." They thought that somehow sin could be transferred by a mere touch. If they should accidentally bump into a sinner, they would rush to the spring of Gihon, remove their clothes and take a ritual bath. They wouldn't approach the temple grounds until they had cleansed themselves. They so hated the thought of even touching a "sinner" that when they walked down the street, they wrapped their robes very tightly around them. They couldn't take the chance that a swishing robe might touch a sinner or a woman or a Gentile!

This explains why the Pharisee saw Jesus' willingness to be touched by a known prostitute as conclusive evidence that He couldn't have any special relationship with God. Yet, Jesus knew his thoughts and said, "Simon, I have something to say to you."

"Teacher, say it," Simon replied.

Jesus then told a story about a man who had two debtors. One fellow owed the man fifty thousand dollars while the other owed him five thousand. When neither borrower could pay what he owed, the lender wrote off both debts. "Tell me, therefore," Jesus said, "which of them will love him more?"

"I suppose the one whom he forgave more," Simon answered.

"You have rightly judged," Jesus said (Luke 7:40-43).

Today, we understand that Jesus intended to draw a spiritual parallel between these fictional financial debts and our own spiritual debts. Some people sin more than others. Some are very moral, always trying to live by the golden rule. They try to be honest, a person of integrity. Sure, they sin, but not much—by comparison, anyway. Meanwhile, others break nearly every rule in the book. They make the sinners' top ten list and get recognized in the Guinness Book of World Records.

But no matter where you might land—whether you've sinned a little or a lot—you are like the men in Jesus' story. You have no funds with which to pay your debt to God, nothing to redeem yourself from your sinful state. Your spiritual bank account reads zero. Jesus used the story to call Simon's attention to his own discourtesy:

> Do you see this woman? I entered your house; you gave Me no water for My feet, but she has washed My feet with her tears and wiped them with the hair of her head. You gave Me no kiss, but this woman has not ceased to kiss My feet since the time I came in. You did not anoint My head with oil, but this woman has anointed My feet with fragrant oil (Luke 7:44-46).

Jesus did not speak like this simply to rebuke Simon. Rather, He had an important point to make: "Therefore I say to you, her sins, which are many, are forgiven, for she loved much. But to whom little is forgiven, the same loves little" (Luke 7:47).

Jesus did not announce how much Simon loved, but you can probably guess.

Are *you* one who loves much or who loves little? Where do you stand? Sometimes it's harder for good people to receive the grace and goodness of God than it is for bad people, because the good ones, like Simon, often don't recognize their need. And thus, when God forgives them, they love only a little.

Have you ever noticed that we don't even want to see God forgive certain people? We think they're just too horrible. We consider their crimes so heinous that we recoil at the thought that God might want to forgive them.

Several years ago after convicted mass murderer Jeffrey Dahmer was converted in jail, newspapers across the country printed irate letters from readers who railed at the idea that he might have accepted Christ while in prison, as reported. How could anyone even *suggest* that such a monster could be in heaven? Some people went so far as to say, "If that animal is in heaven, then I don't want to be there."

Did you know that Charles "Tex" Watson, of the infamous Manson family, has made a profession of faith in Jesus Christ? I've had the opportunity to visit with him in prison. I correspond with him regularly. He has a glowing witness for Jesus Christ and a tremendous love for the Lord. He's been forgiven much, and so it is quite possible that his love far exceeds those who refuse to even acknowledge his faith as genuine. If you know God has forgiven you much, then you love much. If you imagine God has forgiven you little, then you love little.

So then, on a scale of one to ten, where would you rate the love meter in your heart for the Lord? Is it slight or fervent? Large or small? Red-hot or icy-blue? Do you love Him much or love Him little?

Is Your Love for Me Supreme?

Many people lose out in their relationship with the Lord at this very point. They love the Lord, yes—but they love Him only a little. Their interest in other things exceeds their interest in the things of the Lord, and thus they enjoy much less of a relationship with God than what He desires.

God says that your love for Him is to exceed all others. He describes Himself as a jealous God (Exodus 20:5; 1 Corinthians 10:22). He wants your love for Him to rise above all other loves in your life. Your love for Him must reign supremely.

The apostle Peter learned this lesson in a way he would never forget. On the night of Jesus' arrest, Peter denied even knowing the Lord. Afterward, he sank into a depression and perhaps thought his time as a disciple had ended. But then the risen Jesus sought out Peter to reaffirm His love for him—and to give the grieving apostle another opportunity to express his love.

Early one morning on a lonely stretch of shoreline on the Sea of Tiberias, Jesus made breakfast for Peter and six of his buddies who had been fishing. After these men had recovered from the shock of seeing their Savior alive again, Jesus invited them all to eat. And after they had finished eating, He posed a crucial question to Peter.

"Simon Peter, son of Jonah," Jesus said, "do you love Me more than these?" (John 21:15). Just what did Jesus mean by "these"? That's the question. Since the text doesn't make it clear, we cannot be dogmatic. Was Jesus looking at those freshly-caught fish flopping in the net? No doubt Peter loved fishing, as most commercial fishermen do. And so maybe Jesus was asking, "Peter, do you love Me more than your old life of fishing?"

Or perhaps Jesus was looking at the other disciples when He asked His question. At the Last Supper, you'll remember, Jesus had predicted that all His men would desert Him. Peter had boasted, "Even if everyone else abandons You, I never will." It's as if he had said, "Jesus, I love You more than the rest of these fellows. While they may fail You, I never will. You can count on Your boy, Rocky! I'll be there when You need me most. These other guys might be a little flaky, but You can trust me." So perhaps Jesus was referring to Peter's boastful self-comparison with the other disciples.

We don't know what Jesus referred to when He asked Peter, "Do you love Me more than these?" But we really don't have to know. The far more important question is: What are the "these" in our *own* lives?

What things compete in your heart with your love for Jesus? Does your love for those things exceed your love for Jesus? Or does your love for Him rise above all other loves? Is your love for Him paramount? Everything else can go by the wayside; nothing matters as much as your relationship with God. And He calls you to love Him supremely.

Suppose Jesus were having breakfast with you this morning. Imagine that He set down His fork and looked you straight in the eye. If He should ask you, "Do you love Me more than these?" to what might He be referring? What's competing with Him for your love?

With many people it's a relationship, perhaps a romantic attachment to an ungodly person. Perhaps she's asking you to compromise your standards or maybe he's pushing you to go to bed with him. You love this person and don't want to lose him or her. But do you love him more than your relationship with Jesus? Are you willing to sacrifice your relationship with God in order to continue your relationship with her?

Or maybe Jesus is asking you about the "these" of your career. You've set high goals and standards for your life. You're on the way to fulfilling your desires to create a secure financial future. Maybe the opportunity has finally come for that promotion you've been hoping for—but you know that this new assignment may require questionable business practices. You've been told that at this level, you have to do some unsavory things in order to keep the clients happy. Jesus might well be asking you, "Do you love Me more than your fondest ambition? Do you love Me more than those goals or the fulfilling of your dreams?"

Of course, there's nothing wrong with having moral relationships and activities and possessions that you deeply enjoy. There's nothing wrong with fishing or romance or pursuing a career. These things become wrong only when your love for them exceeds your love for the Lord. When they become the greatest love of your life—when you become willing to sacrifice your relationship with God in order to indulge these other passions—then they have ceased to be good for you.

Jesus asks you today, "Do you love Me more than these? Or am I somewhere down the priority list? Does your love for Me exceed all other interests and all other loves in your life? Am I first? Do you love Me supremely?"

It's easy to glibly answer, "Lord, You know I love You more than anything else in all the world!" Peter did that. But when it comes down to practical realities, is that just an empty profession? Or is there real weight to it?

Of Love and Hate

What does it mean to love God supremely? Jesus made a startling comparison in Luke 14 that both clarifies the issue and confuses a lot of readers.

"If anyone comes to Me," He said, "and does not hate his father and mother, wife and children, brothers and sisters … he cannot be My disciple" (Luke 14:26). You see the problem; don't you? Here we have been talking about the love of God and loving Him supremely, and now Jesus starts talking about hate as a *good* thing.

Fortunately, the problem is easy to overcome. We struggle because in the United States, our words *love* and *hate* lie at opposite extremes. They are opposed to one another. In the Middle Eastern mind and thought, however, they serve as comparative words, not opposite words. So Jesus is not commanding us to hate everyone who means a great deal to us; in fact, He's saying that our love for them must pale in comparison to our love for God. We should love God so supremely that any other love looks like hate by comparison.

You can be sure He's not instructing you to actually hate anyone because the Bible explicitly commands the contrary:

- "Love your enemies" (Luke 6:27).
- "A new commandment I give to you, that you love one another" (John 13:34).
- "Husbands, love your wives, just as Christ also loved the church" (Ephesians 5:25).
- "Greater love has no one than this, than to lay down one's life for his friends" (John 15:13).

Obviously, Jesus is not saying that to follow Him you must hate your mother and your father, your sisters, your brothers, your family members, your children, and your friends. He is saying that your love for Him must exceed your love for your mother, your father, or your wife, or your children, or your brothers and your sisters, or your friends. Your love for Him must reign supremely.

That means that if your parents tell you, "It's either your love for Jesus or your love for us," then you must choose to love Jesus. If your wife says, "I'm not going to stay with you anymore if you insist on this Christian obsession," then your love for Jesus has to exceed your love for your wife. If your husband says, "I cannot stand this religious stuff anymore! If you keep it up, I'm leaving," then you must let him leave. Paul wrote, "If the unbeliever departs, let him depart; a brother or a sister is not under bondage in such cases" (1 Corinthians 7:15). Your love for Jesus has to be first and paramount.

Matthew's gospel makes this intense comparison very clear. There Jesus says, "He who loves father or mother more than Me is not worthy of Me. And he who loves son or daughter more than Me is not worthy of Me" (Matthew 10:37). So don't worry that to love God supremely you must start hating your wife, kids, and anybody else you hold dear. Not so! God instructs you to love them, and through His Spirit He enables you to do so; nevertheless, your love for the Lord must rise above every other love.

Even More Than You

It sounds pretty extreme that Jesus would say your love for God must make your love for friends and family look like hate; doesn't it? How radical!

And then Jesus goes the extra mile.

"If anyone comes to Me and does not hate … his own life also, he cannot be My disciple. And whoever does not bear his cross and come after Me cannot be My disciple" (Luke 14:26-27). Now He says you're to love Him even more than you love yourself. That's really loving God a lot; isn't it?

Once more, we know He doesn't mean you need to literally hate yourself. In the first place, that would be impossible, according to Paul: "For no one ever hated his own flesh, but nourishes and cherishes it, just as the Lord does the church" (Ephesians 5:29). For another, Jesus Himself quoted part of the Great Commandment like this: "You shall love your neighbor as yourself" (Matthew 22:39). God assumes that we all love ourselves; that's how He designed us. Nevertheless, our love for ourselves is to seem like hate in comparison to our love for God.

And what are we to think of His statement about the need for a true disciple to "bear his cross"? Many ridiculous things have been said over the years concerning this idea. You've probably heard someone say: "I have a mother-in-law who really likes to nag. I hate it every time we have to go to her house—but I guess that's just the cross I have to bear." No, no, no, no, *no*! That's not the cross.

Or someone else says, "I have this arthritic toe and I guess that's just the cross I have to bear." No! In the life of Jesus, the cross represented a total submission to the will of the Father. In the garden of Gethsemane, Jesus prayed, "O My Father, if it is possible, let this cup [the crucifixion] pass from Me; nevertheless, not as I will, but as You will" (Matthew 26:39). *That's* the cross. The cross is the complete surrendering of yourself to the will of God.

Such a total surrendering of your will might involve suffering. It might involve pain. It might even include your premature death—and no one will ever willingly make such a choice without first nurturing a love for God that exceeds all others. Without such a love, such discipleship cannot exist. With such a love, it cannot help but exist.

It's a Choice

Some people may respond, "Well, that sort of passion is fine for people who are built for it. Great for them! But God didn't put me together like that. Frankly, it's beyond me."

You want to know a secret? It's beyond me, too—frankly, it's beyond all of us—in the natural. Left to ourselves, none of us could love God like this. But in His love, God doesn't leave us to ourselves. He sends His Spirit to live inside of us so that we might start living beyond the natural, in the realm of the supernatural. When we try to love God in our own strength, the Bible says, "Are you not carnal and behaving like mere men?" (1 Corinthians 3:3). But when we choose to live by the Spirit, it says to us, "Keep yourselves in the love of God" (Jude 1:21).

You see, God loves you and because He loves you, He wants to bless you. He wants to bestow His goodness upon your life. Unfortunately, it is possible for you to get out of the place of God's blessing, just as the children of Israel did through unbelief. Their sin kept them from entering into the full blessings that God had intended for them. In a similar way, through pride and rebellion against God, you can keep yourself from the full blessings that God wants to bestow upon you. So Jude instructs, "keep yourselves in the love of God." It's a choice.

God will never say, "Would you look at the way he's living! I won't love him anymore." No! God will still love you, but He weeps over your sin. He won't do for you what He wants to do when your life becomes inconsistent with His nature and His ways.

Like Cain, if you allow hatred to fill your heart, God cannot bless you.

Like Balaam, if you allow greed to fill your heart, God cannot bless you.

Like Korah, if you allow jealousy to master your life, God cannot do for you what He really wants to do.

So keep yourself in the love of God. Keep yourself in the place where God can do all He wants to do for you because of His infinite love.

Here's the Joy!

Remember my shiny new convertible? The beauty that somebody dented before I even drove it home? It turns out the thing really did burn.

Years later I got a letter from the Department of Motor Vehicles asking if I knew anything about that car. As soon as I got a free moment, I called the DMV to say, "Sorry, I sold that car years ago."

A state employee on the other end of the line replied, "Well, it's been abandoned on the highway. The engine blew up on it."

As I put down the phone, I could almost hear the words that the Lord spoke to me so many years before. As I drove home from the market, steaming, I had felt Him asking me, "Where's all the joy and the glory and the blessing and the love that you were talking about just a few moments ago?" One little ding—on a now-burned up car—had sent me from, "Oh, Lord, You're so good! I love You *so* much!" to "God, I hate people!"

Had the apostle John been riding with me, he might have tapped me on the shoulder and said, "Uh, Chuck? I hate to say this to you, but I think you're a liar. Because anyone who says, 'I love God,' but hates his brother, is a liar" (1 John 4:20).

We prove our love for Jesus by obeying Him—and He has said very clearly, "This is My commandment, that you love one another as I have loved you" (John 15:12).

Dings on new convertibles or not. Considerate drivers or not.

"Do you love Me more than these?" Jesus wants to know. "Does your love for Me reign supremely?" Only you—and He—know the answer.

A Rekindled Heart

THE BLOOM OF FIRST love is such a beautiful thing. It gives a special fragrance to your entire life. You don't want to eat. You don't want to sleep. You desire to savor every last thought of the one you love.

Remember that first love you had for the Lord when you discovered His amazing love for you? Surely, you recall that sweet feeling when He first lifted the heavy guilt of sin off your back, when you first realized that Jesus loved you so much that He died for you. Your heart naturally responded to that love. In those days, no sacrifice seemed too great to make for the Lord. In fact, you didn't even consider it a sacrifice. Anything you could do for the Lord felt like sheer joy. Remember the reckless abandonment of your life to Jesus because you loved Him so much?

Some time ago I had a conversation with the members of the music group *Love Song*—one of the most popular bands of the Jesus Movement. We recalled the early days after they had first come to the Lord. They willingly traveled anywhere, just to sing for Jesus Christ. They had an old van and all they needed was a box of raisins, a pack of oats and some trail mix, and these guys could go on forever. They were willing and eager to go because they loved the Lord so much. The excitement of doing *something* for Jesus energized their happy, hippy hearts.

How long has it been since you felt a similar bloom of first love for Jesus? Has it been a while? Can you still remember? Too often, the march of life has a way of trampling our early experiences of joy and enthusiasm in Jesus. Bills come due. Illness intrudes. Relationships sour. Cars break down. Tragedy strikes. And before we know it, our love for Jesus shrinks to a cold, dry shell of what it had been before we knew the Lord.

And God weeps.

The Tears of God

You can almost feel God's tears when He asks His straying people, "What injustice have your fathers found in Me, that they have gone far from Me, have followed idols, and have become idolaters?" And you clearly hear His anguish when He says,

> Be astonished, O heavens, at this, and be horribly afraid; be very desolate. For My people have committed two evils: they have forsaken Me, the fountain of living waters, and hewn themselves cisterns—broken cisterns that can hold no water (Jeremiah 2:5, 12-13).

The Lord lamented over ancient Israel because His people had left Him, their only source of life, in a futile attempt to find satisfaction in the things of the flesh. Predictably, they had become empty.

So often in history, we have seen this sad pattern repeated. Men and women have sought after God and found Him. They began their lives of faith with great joy and excitement, but gradually their devotion waned until they turned their backs on the Lord and walked away.

The reasons behind such spiritual wandering vary: misfortune, busyness, heartache, greed, disappointment, ambition, carelessness, and countless more—but the cure is always the same. There's only one. We must allow the Lord to reignite our hearts for Him, that once more we might warm ourselves in the glow of His love. As God told His wandering people so long ago:

> I will give them a heart to know Me, that I am the Lord; and they shall be My people, and I will be their God, for they shall return to Me with their whole heart (Jeremiah 24:7).

So may it be with each of us.

Suffering for Jesus

Many people lose their love for Jesus when life beats them up. They begin on a high note, but soon stop singing when the air gets trampled out of their chest.

Their lives flow along much like Psalm 44, which starts out with tremendous spiritual confidence and ends in a terrible dilemma. The writer goes from, "In God we boast all day long, and praise Your name forever," to "Why do You sleep, O Lord? Arise! Do not cast us off forever"—all in the space of fifteen short verses.

The apostle Paul noticed this drift. He quotes one verse of Psalm 44 in the eighth chapter of Romans, where he describes the glorious position of believers in Christ. He asks several questions designed to increase our spiritual confidence: "If God is for us, who can be against us?" (Romans 8:31). "Who shall bring a charge against God's elect? It is God who justifies. Who is he who condemns? It is Christ who died, and furthermore is also risen, who is even at the right hand of God, who also makes intercession for us. Who shall separate us from the love of Christ?" (vv. 33-35).

Such tremendous encouragement. And yet then the apostle writes, "As it is written: 'For Your sake we are killed all day long; we are accounted as sheep for the slaughter'" (Romans 8:36). This quote comes from Psalm 44:22—and it sounds a bit odd, doesn't it, especially in this context? Discordant, like someone hit a sour note in the flute section. And yet Paul insists that the Conductor has directed each note.

The early Christians went through heavy persecution despite their love for God. In fact, it was *because* of their love for God that they were persecuted. It was *because* of their faith in Jesus Christ that they were placed on the racks, that they were fed to the lions, and that they were burned at the stake.

Here's an uncomfortable truth we need to understand if we are to keep our hearts burning for the Lord: God has not promised us a bed of roses in this life. He has promised us a glorious eternal life with Him in His kingdom, but walking with Him down here is not a popular walk. It's not going to make you the favorite of the worldly crowd. At times it's going to be deeply unpopular and it's going to take real courage to live for Jesus Christ. And you are not going to understand many of the unpleasant things that transpire. You must trust Him and continue to commit yourself to Him.

The apostle Peter had to learn this tough lesson. Jesus told him, "Most assuredly, I say to you, when you were younger, you girded yourself and walked where you wished; but when you are old, you will stretch out your hands, and another will gird you and carry you where you do not wish" (John 21:18). John explains to readers of his gospel, "This He spoke, signifying by what death he would glorify God" (v. 19).

Jesus thus predicted that Peter's arms would one day get stretched out on a cross. Peter would die as the Lord did, by crucifixion. Tradition tells us that when Peter was about to be executed in Rome, he requested that he be crucified upside down because he felt unworthy to be crucified as his Lord. Long before that happened, however, Jesus told Peter what following Him would cost: "It's going to cost you your life, Peter. They're going to crucify you."

The Lord didn't say, "If you just follow Me, Pete, your life is going to be surrounded by roses and pleasant experiences. In no time at all you'll enter into a glorious bliss. You'll have no problems, no worries, no difficulties. Things are going to be so smooth and nice for you!" Not at all. Instead the Lord told him, "It's a rough road ahead, Peter. The world is going to hate you. They hated Me and you're not greater than your Lord. You'll be persecuted for My sake. You'll be thrown into prison. Even your own family will turn against you. And then you'll be put to death." Jesus laid it out straight for the cost of following Him. And as strange as it may seem, He did this to give Peter strength, not to take it away from him.

From the Bible's perspective, suffering is what makes your following Jesus all the more meaningful. *It proves your love*. The fact that you're willing to experience these difficulties and hardships in order to develop your relationship with Him cements the love relationship you have with God. It's something like Job said: "Though He slay me, yet will I trust Him" (Job 13:15).

Peter, of course, didn't like the sound of this. Who would? So when he looked around and saw John, he asked Jesus, "But Lord, what about this man?" (John: 21:21). Jesus did not hesitate. "If I will that he remain till I come, what is that to you? You follow Me" (v. 22). In other words, "Peter, he's none of your business. Your business is to follow My lead. The only commitment you need to worry about is your own."

The Lord always deals with you and me on a personal basis. He's interested in *you*. And so Jesus says, "What difference does it make to you what I choose to do with My own servants? You follow Me. *That's* your business. I'll take care of the others. You follow Me."

If you want to keep your heart on fire for God, you really have no choice but to keep your eyes on Jesus, instead of those around you.

We Had Hoped

The scene is the very first Easter Sunday morning, the day Jesus rose from the dead. Two discouraged disciples trudge along a lonely road, heading to a small village about seven miles outside of Jerusalem.

One man is named Cleopas. We don't know anything about him except his name; if he ever did anything of note for the Lord, it wasn't recorded. We don't even know the name of the other one. So here we have an unknown disciple and an unnamed one—just plain disciples.

Yet Jesus spent more time with these two ordinary disciples on the day of His resurrection than He did with all of the apostles. Earlier that morning He had a very short visit with Mary Magdalene. A little later He met a few other women as they left the empty tomb. Some time that morning He met with Peter; we don't know anything about that meeting except that He appeared. I think He just wanted to encourage Peter and let him know that he was forgiven. But with these two unknown disciples, Jesus spent a good part of the afternoon.

When we first meet these two disciples, they are walking from Jerusalem to Emmaus, a trip of a little under seven miles. You can imagine how long it would take them to walk that far, feeling so down-cast and discouraged knowing that Jesus Christ, their Savior, had been crucified. They had no hope for the future; they saw no reason to go on living.

Just a few days earlier they had a burning passion for the things of the Lord, believing Jesus was going to establish God's kingdom on earth. They were expecting the world soon to be filled with peace and love. Men of greed would be dethroned! Righteousness would reign! Wars would cease and suffering would end! They anticipated the coming of the glorious kingdom of God, promised in the Scriptures when the Messiah arrived—for they had come to identify Jesus as the Messiah.

But when they saw Jesus hanging on the cross and watched Him take His last breath, all of their hopes for the kingdom of God on earth went as limp as their Lord's dead body. The flame went out. Their burning passion for the immediate establishment of God's kingdom had died.

As they walked along the road, they felt sad, dejected, hopeless. Despair filled their hearts. And then an incognito Jesus catches up with them and begins to walk with them. "Why do you fellows look so sad?" He asked. "You seem to be so troubled as you walk along."

One disciple asked Him, "Are You the only stranger in Jerusalem who doesn't know the things that have been happening here the last few days?"

"What things?" Jesus asked—as if He didn't know!

The Lord loves to draw us out with questions. He asks them, not because He doesn't know the answers but because we don't. Sometimes as we express ourselves, we come to a much clearer understanding of what's going on inside of us. And so the Lord invited these two discouraged disciples to express their despair, their sorrow, their problems.

In response, these disciples began to tell Him all about Jesus of Nazareth. They called Him a mighty prophet in both deeds and words before God and all the people. No man like Jesus had ever walked this planet. No man had ever alleviated such suffering. No man had ever brought more hope. No man had inspired others to more noble deeds than this Man.

"But the chief priests and rulers delivered Him up to be condemned and crucified," they sighed. "But we had hoped He would be the One to redeem Israel." A fire had blazed in their hearts as they waited for Jesus to set up His kingdom, but that fire had burned out three days ago when the Romans hung Him on a cross.

While they reported some women had come from the tomb earlier that morning telling of a stone rolled back and two angels claiming Jesus had risen, they had passed it off as the talk of excitable women. Still, they had gone to the tomb to see for themselves. They saw the stone rolled away and the place where Jesus' body had lain, but they didn't see Him. Even the empty tomb didn't dispel their hopelessness. They didn't believe He had risen. And so they told Jesus how their hopes had crashed and burned.

Now it was Jesus' turn to speak. "Oh slow of heart to believe all that the prophets have spoken," He said. And He began to unfold the Scriptures to them.

Do you know their problem? They believed only a part of the story. The Old Testament contains hundreds of prophecies of Jesus. The Scriptures speak of a Messiah who would come to reign on the throne of David, bringing peace to the whole earth. These prophecies predict the end of wars when men will beat their swords into plowshares and their spears into pruning hooks. They speak of a glorious day when greed will disappear and all people will live together in love and harmony. Crime—gone. Sickness—gone. Corruption—gone. And these men had hoped that this day had come. They believed Jesus was the long-anticipated Messiah. They had expected Him to do all the things the Bible had promised the Messiah would do.

But that was only part of the truth! Other Scriptures spoke of the Messiah's suffering, of His rejection, and crucifixion. These men either hadn't seen or didn't believe those Scriptures—and that's why they felt so confused after the death of Jesus. They didn't believe *all* that the prophets had spoken concerning Him. And so Jesus began to take these ordinary disciples through the Word of God, from Moses through the prophets, declaring to them all that the Bible had prophesied about the Messiah.

Jesus perhaps showed them the ugly scene at the beginning of humankind's sin. God told Satan that the "seed of the woman"—that is, the

Messiah—would "bruise" the devil's "head," but that the serpent would "bruise" the "heel" of the seed of the woman—a shadowy prophecy about the victory of Christ on the cross (see Genesis 3:15).

A little later in Genesis, Jesus probably illustrated the story of how God commanded Abraham to sacrifice his beloved son Isaac. Perhaps He described how they journeyed for three days from Hebron to Mount Moriah, and how Isaac pointed out that they lacked a sacrificial animal, and Abraham had replied, "God will provide Himself a sacrifice, my son. In the Mount of the Lord it shall be seen" (22:8, 14). Then maybe Jesus noted that Mount Moriah was the same place where God had just given His Son to be the sacrifice for the sins of the whole world.

Envision Jesus taking them into the book of Exodus and reminding them of the famous story of Israel's deliverance from bondage in Egypt. That on one fateful night the angel of God passed through the land to slay the firstborn of every household—except those households where the family had slain a lamb from their flock and put its blood into a basin, and then with a little hyssop bush, sprinkled the blood on the doorposts and lintel. Maybe Jesus mentioned that the applied blood formed a cross. And surely He explained how Jesus, as the Lamb of God, fulfilled the type of the Passover lamb.

Maybe next Jesus took these disciples into Leviticus and explained the real significance of the sin offering and the trespass offering, and why the shedding of blood was required for the remission of sins. Quite possibly He revealed how all these things pointed toward that single, once-and-for-all sacrifice that God offered for the sins of the human race.

Undoubtedly, Jesus opened up the Psalms, perhaps Psalm 16, where God promised He would not leave the soul of His Holy One in hell nor allow Him to see corruption. Or maybe Jesus moved right to Psalm 22 where David predicted the Messiah was to be poured out like water, with all of His bones out of joint—as in a crucifixion. He probably highlighted the prophecy that His enemies would pierce His hands and His feet and cast lots for His clothing.

Then on to Isaiah 50, where the prophet says the Messiah would give His back to the smiters and His cheeks to those who would pull out His beard. Then perhaps forward to Isaiah 52, which declared His face would be so marred He could not be recognized as a human being. Then certainly on to Isaiah 53 where the prophet drew a picture of the Messiah despised and rejected by men, a man of sorrows and acquainted with grief. "But surely He was wounded for our transgressions and bruised for our iniquities … by His stripes we are healed … He poured out His life unto death and was numbered with the transgressors."

Maybe Jesus expounded to these men the prophet Daniel, who had predicted the very time the Messiah would come—483 years after the commandment went forth to rebuild Jerusalem. Also disclosing how the Messiah would be killed and would not immediately receive His kingdom.

Closing with Zechariah, perhaps, where Jesus might have shown them how the Messiah would be traded for thirty pieces of silver, with money later thrown down in the temple and used to buy a potter's field.

Jesus systematically went through the entire Old Testament, from Moses through the prophets, explaining *all* the Scriptures regarding Himself—not just those of the glorious reign of the Messiah, but also of His suffering and His death.

As the disciples reached Emmaus with Jesus, I imagine they felt surprised: "Emmaus already? My, the time went by fast!" Jesus acted as though He were going to walk further, but they said, "Oh no, it's getting late, much too late to travel. Stay with us; why don't You?" And so they urged Him to remain. Soon after He came into the house with them, He broke some bread—and suddenly they recognized Him.

"It's Jesus!" they cried. But no sooner did they recognize Him than He disappeared, leaving them with rekindled hearts and a wondrous report for the apostles. You can be sure it took them far less time to return to Jerusalem than it did to get to Emmaus! And they said to each other, "Did not our hearts burn within us while He talked with us along the path as He opened to us the Scriptures?"

Jesus had rekindled the flame. It had gone out because they did not understand the ways of God and the purposes of God. Faced with this great problem—a tremendous difficulty that they did not understand—they had allowed the flame to go out.

Why No Gospel of Cleopas?

Oh, how I wish Cleopas would have written down what he had heard that day! I wish we had in our Bibles the gospel of Cleopas, containing only the message of Jesus on the road to Emmaus. What I wouldn't give to have Jesus' exposition of all the Scriptures that pertained to Him!

But for some reason, God deemed fit not to record it for us.

Could it be that He wants us to dig it out for ourselves? Maybe He doesn't want to simply hand it to us on a silver platter; we're already too lazy for that! Perhaps the Lord just wants us to work for it a bit.

Or maybe there's an even greater reason. Maybe He wants to walk with you along the path when you get discouraged, when the flame is going out. Maybe He simply wants to do for you what He did for the two disciples heading to Emmaus, just personally open to you all of those Scriptures.

I know that some of the greatest experiences of my life are those times when the Lord comes to me and begins to open up the Scriptures. Suddenly I see them in a new light. I gain a new insight and understanding. How thrilling it is! Oh, I get excited.

Certainly, I can become discouraged, just like the two disciples. Maybe I have built my hopes on a particular relationship or on a specific event, and I get excited as everything looks to be coming together. "This is going to do it!" I cry. And then things fall apart. As they crumble, I moan, "Oh no, it's all over. Now it will never happen." The flame seems to flicker out and I feel utterly dejected. A coldness comes over my mind and heart as I harden myself to life and my circumstances. I feel life has dealt me a bitter blow. I had hope, but the hope has died. The flame has gone out.

Jesus saw His disciples in exactly that same condition. And what had brought them to that place? They didn't know *all* the Scriptures. They didn't have *all* the truth. If they had known the whole truth, they wouldn't have grown so discouraged.

So often we rush to judgment, armed with just half the story. We don't see the full plan of God. We don't see what God is working out. We don't see the end result to which God is bringing us. And because we see only half the story, we let the flame go out and then feel totally discouraged.

"There is no hope," we say, "no sense in trying to go on." Why do we speak like that? Because we are looking at only half of the story.

Jesus opened to them *all* the Scriptures. He let them see the whole story, and in seeing the whole story, the flame reignited and their hearts began to burn once more: "Didn't our hearts begin to burn in us as He talked with us along the way and opened up the Scriptures?" Jesus rekindled their hope by opening to them the Word of God.

Maybe you feel discouraged right now. Perhaps you have lost hope and the flame has gone out. Jesus says to you, "Your love has burned low—but do you remember when you first came to Me? You'd come an hour early to church, just so you could sit in the front row. You couldn't get enough. Oh, how the flame blazed inside!"

But somehow—maybe through some disappointment, some unfortunate experience that you couldn't understand, or some other difficulty—the flame began to flicker, then die. And now you feel a coldness, a numbness. The passion is gone.

The Lord wants to relight that fire. He wants His Holy Spirit to blow on those embers and rekindle that flame. He longs to renew your love and passion for Him by walking with you through the Scriptures.

Take the Challenge

I challenge you to get alone with the Word of God. Sit down and begin to read it again and see if Jesus won't come alongside you and open up the Bible to you. Let Him expound the Scriptures and give you understanding about the things that have brought such discouragement to your heart.

Jesus is keenly interested in you! He's interested in all those who have lost hope. He's especially interested in rekindling in your heart a blazing fire of love for God that may have burned low or gone out.

Remember the marvelous hope you have for the future, a home in the beautiful kingdom of God where you will dwell in His presence. At His right hand there is fullness of joy and pleasures forevermore.

In the meantime, as you make your way through this pilgrimage on earth, you must expect times of discouragement, for you don't fully understand God's ways. On this side of eternity, you will always have an incomplete knowledge of what happens. So you must look for encouragement in His Word, praying that He'll help you and sustain you, reminding you of your hope of a permanent home in His blessed kingdom.

Get It Back

What a beautiful thing first love is! We've all experienced its excitement. We've all tasted of the warm, glowing feeling we have all over just because we're in love. The Lord says He misses that. And He would like for you to have it back.

It's possible, because His love for you doesn't change. It doesn't wane through time. It doesn't grow cold. His love for you is just as fervent as when you first discovered it.

God hasn't moved! So if something's out of place in our love, it's you and I who have moved. We are the ones who need to repent for the estrangement. So let us pray that God would draw us to Himself again by His Holy Spirit.

Rekindle our hearts, Lord! And may we respond to Your Word and go forth loving You like never before.

A Transformed Heart

WHEN CALVARY CHAPEL FIRST began growing rapidly, at times I had no idea what to do with it. Never in my life had I pastored a large congregation, yet suddenly here I was becoming the pastor of a large church.

Many times when I stopped long enough to consider what was happening, I would get really shaken up inside. *What in the world are we going to do?* I worried. *What has the Lord gotten me into?*

I simply wasn't prepared for the challenge. I would say, "Lord, what are You doing? What if *this* should happen? What if *that* should happen?"

At those times the Lord would often speak to my heart. "Whose church is this?" He would ask.

"Well, it's Your church," I would reply.

"Then why are you worried?"

"I don't know," I'd say.

So I would throw the problem over onto Him. I'd say, "Okay. It's Your church, Lord, Your problems. You handle them."

I doubt that I could have survived any other way. If I had tried to carry the weight of all the problems and challenges facing us, it would have wiped me out. The Lord had to transform my thinking. I had to learn that it's His church.

And what if disaster struck?

"Hey, it's His church."

What if we went bankrupt?

"It's His."

What if we went belly-up?

"Again, His problem."

God didn't allow any of those things to happen; praise His name. And He continues to be the head of the body, His church. I've learned to enjoy the ride—not to worry, not to fret, not to get anxious. I say, "Lord, it's Your church. In Your time and in Your way, go ahead and do what You want with it."

Do you know that's one of the best ways we have to show the Lord that we love Him? When we refuse to worry and instead put our full trust in God, we demonstrate our genuine love for Him. Of course, we can only demonstrate such love if God first does a work of transformation within us. It takes a transformed heart to love God to the utmost.

The Work of Prayer

In prayer, God can change our whole attitude about a situation. In just the time it takes to bring our concerns to Him in prayer, the Lord can transform our hearts. He can bring confidence to our souls and new resolve to our spirits. As we pray, we often get a new perspective—heaven's perspective—on the situations that confront us.

In the very early days of Calvary Chapel, I often imagined I was alone. I thought I was in this fight by myself. Sometimes I thought the Lord had forsaken me—but as I prayed, I found new assurance that God is on the throne. My faith received a lift and my confidence returned as I realized once more, *God is going to take care of it!*

David knew this kind of transforming experience through prayer. Nobody ever questions David's love for God—and yet when he found himself in tight spots, his devotion and confidence often wavered, just as ours does. And how did he regain his trust in God and his love for his Savior? Most often, he did it through prayer.

David began Psalm 13 in absolute desperation: "How long, O Lord? Will You forget me forever? How long will You hide Your face from me?" (v.1). He carries on like this for several verses, but then his praying starts to change his heart. And by the end of his prayer he's singing quite a different tune than the one that began his petition: "But I have trusted in Your mercy; my heart shall rejoice in Your salvation. I will sing to the Lord, because He has dealt bountifully with me" (vv. 5-6).

If we want to love God with all of our hearts, we need transformed hearts. And prayer is one of the primary tools we have to cooperate with God in this key process of transformation. Oh, the mighty changes wrought through prayer!

God's Commandments: Easy or Hard?

The Bible provides us with an easy test to determine how well we are cooperating with God's Spirit in the transformation of our hearts.

How much do we really love God? The apostle John provides us with the quiz:

> For this is the love of God, that we keep His commandments. And His commandments are not burdensome (1 John 5:3).

It's one thing to say that we prove our love for God by keeping His commandments. It's quite another to say that those commandments "are not burdensome." Some people think they surely are.

For example, you may think that it is very difficult and almost impossible to love your fellow believers as God commands. Maybe there's one person in particular that you just cannot stand. God still says you are to love that person. "And you're telling me that's not hard?" you ask.

The truth is, loving each other as we love ourselves can be very difficult; in fact, it takes a work of God's Spirit within our hearts. When I have to deal with someone I don't particularly like, I know I cannot simply say, "I'm just going to love him."

I've tried that. I've attempted to reason with myself saying: "He's not such a bad guy. He's got some good traits and I know I shouldn't feel that way about him. He may be loud and brash and he says stupid things, but really, he's not that bad. He's not horrid. I can tolerate him." It's like we used to say when we were kids: "I love you only enough to get to heaven."

But then this man shows up at a party. As he comes in—loud-mouthed, crude, and saying some stupid thing—I think, *Oh, why didn't you just stay at home?* And all of my good intentions go out the window. All my efforts at bringing my mind into a loving state disappear in a tiny puff of smoke.

Yes, it's true; you are simply incompatible with some people. They're probably too much like you! It's amazing how horrible my sins look when someone else is committing them. When I commit them, they don't seem so bad. But if someone else starts committing them, well, they look ugly and horrible. I cannot stand that person!

To love others as we love ourselves—which proves our love for God—takes a special work of God's Spirit within us. We cannot do it. We cannot manufacture *agape* love. We cannot psyche ourselves into *agape* love. And that's why the existence of such love in our hearts provides proof that it's really from God.

God has given me a love for people whom I could not stand in the natural. When I experience God's love working in me, changing my heart and transforming my attitude, I know it's God's love being perfected in me. Many times I've had to pray, "Lord, I know You require me to love this guy—but that's impossible for me. I cannot do it. But Lord, I want You to work in me and give me Your love for him. I know that I don't love him, but I know that You do. So give me Your love for him."

It's extremely important that we be totally frank with God in these matters because He knows the truth, anyway. Many times we try to con God with our prayers: "Oh God, thank You for this great love that You have given to me for everyone! Now Lord, there's one fellow whom I'm having difficulty loving with the intensity and degree that I should be loving him. So Lord, increase the intensity of my love." How phony! When you're not honest with God, He cannot do anything for you. You need to be straightforward and frank with God.

So you say, "God, I hate him. I can't stand his looks or anything else about him. And so, God, if there is going to be any love flowing toward him from my direction, You're going to have to supply it. But I'm willing, Lord, for You to do it. Please work within my heart. Take away my hatred and give me Your love. Transform me into the likeness of Jesus."

When you're honest, God can work with you and deal with the problem. But so long as you try to delude yourself, you won't get anywhere. God knows the truth of your heart—and He knows it needs a work of transformation from the inside out.

External Versus Internal

The Ten Commandments spelled out God's conditions to receive His blessing and to enjoy the benefit of being His people. We call it "the old covenant," and it failed. Not on God's part, but on our part. So it was necessary that God establish a new covenant.

Hebrews chapter 8 tells us of this new covenant. The writer quotes from Jeremiah 31, where God said,

> Behold, the days are coming, says the Lord, when I will make a new covenant with the house of Israel and with the house of Judah—not according to the covenant that I made with their fathers in the day when I took them by the hand to lead them out of the land of Egypt; because they did not continue in My covenant, and I disregarded them, says the Lord. For this is the covenant that I will make with the house of Israel after those days, says the Lord: I will put My laws in their mind and write them on their hearts; and I will be their God, and they shall be My people (Hebrews 8:8-10).

In this new covenant, God works from within. He changes our heart and transforms our mind. So the basic difference between the old covenant and the new covenant is that the old covenant rested on the people's ability to obey external rules, while the new covenant depends on God's work within our hearts to transform us from the inside out.

Jesus Christ established this new covenant through His work on the cross, as He said at the Last Supper: "This is My body which is given for you; do this in remembrance of Me.... This cup is the new covenant in My blood, which is shed for you" (Luke 22:19-20). Through Jesus Christ, God established a new covenant that makes possible a transformed life. As you walk with Jesus, God makes you a new person from the inside out.

That is why Paul wrote to the Colossians, "Do not lie to one another, since you have put off the old man with his deeds, and have put on the new man who is renewed in knowledge according to the image of Him who created him" (Colossians 3:9-10).

And it explains why he wrote to the Philippians,

> Therefore, my beloved, as you have always obeyed, not as in my presence only, but now much more in my absence, work out your own salvation with fear and trembling; for it is God who works in you both to will and to do for His good pleasure (Philippians 2:12-13).

Since the time of Jesus, God works from within. He changes your mind and your heart. He gives you a new will that desires to please Him, that desires to do His work, that desires to obey Him, so that your own heart desires to love and serve the Lord. God changes you from within so that you do the things that you love to do.

Some people read Psalm 37 and get really pumped, but for all the wrong reasons. They read verse 4—"Delight yourself also in the Lord, and He shall give you the desires of your heart"—and mistakenly think, *Whoa! All I have to do is delight myself in the Lord and I can have a new Mercedes! I can live in a bay-front home on Balboa Island! Oh my Lord, You bet I delight myself in You!*

No, no, that's not what it's saying. It's saying, "If you delight yourself in the Lord, He will put *His* desires in your heart. He will write His law on your heart so that doing the will of God will become the delight and the joy of your life." Then you will be able to say, along with the psalmist, "I delight to do Your will, O my God, and Your law is within my heart" (Psalm 40:8).

As God transforms you from within, He plants His desires in your heart so that you delight to do His will. There's nothing you want more, nothing you like better than doing the will of God. It becomes your longing, your desire, your love. He puts His desires in your heart and then blesses you for acting on them. How can you lose?

Don't Live in Sin

When Jesus comes into your heart by faith, He dwells within you and from there He begins to transform you. The old things of the flesh start to fall off and you begin living a life after the Spirit.

That means that if you are truly a child of God, you can no longer live in sin. Oh, you might occasionally fall back into the mud, but you won't lie there and wallow in it. The Spirit of Jesus within you convicts you and puts you back on the right path whenever you stumble and fall. He works from the inside to bring you back into a right relationship with the Lord. It's God working within you, not you working hard on the outside to perfect your fallen flesh.

So Jude writes, "Now to Him who is able to keep you from stumbling" (v. 24). You see it; don't you? Personal transformation doesn't depend upon your ability. The first covenant failed because sinful human beings couldn't hold up their end of the bargain. But the second covenant will stand forever because of "Him who is able to keep you from stumbling, and to present you faultless before the presence of His glory with exceeding joy, to God our Savior, who alone is wise, be glory and majesty, dominion and power, both now and forever. Amen" (vv. 24-25).

It is *God* who enables you to love the Lord supremely as He works within you to transform your heart.

The Objection

Some people hesitate to enter into the Christian life because they say, "I just cannot live up to Christian standards. I'd like to be a Christian, but I just cannot give up my booze." Or they may say, "I'd like to be a Christian, but I just cannot give up my women." Or "I'd like to be a Christian, but I like the excitement I get when I view pornography." They list all sorts of things that they feel they just cannot give up.

Invariably, these things have captivated them and now hold them hostage. These individuals may really long for a pure, better life—they may even long to be freed from these things—but whenever they've tried to free themselves, they've failed. And thus they find themselves longing and fearing at the same time, because they know their own weaknesses.

Now, it's true that they cannot give up those old things on their own; but it's also true that when they place their faith in Christ, it's no longer their ability at issue, but God's. These old things will just start falling off when they enter this new covenant with God. It isn't a matter of driving out the darkness, as we are so prone to think.

When you go into a dark room, do you take a bat with you and swing at the darkness, hoping to drive it out? Of course not. You just flip the light switch. When the light comes on, it automatically dispels the darkness. To light a room you depend upon the dispelling force of the greater power.

When the light of Jesus' love turns on in your heart, the darkness has to go. It simply cannot coexist with the Light. So the idea isn't to drive out the darkness, but to allow Jesus, the Light of the world, to come into your heart and lighten up everything within. His presence will automatically dispel the darkness.

And it even gets better. The Lord replaces that old, corrupted stuff with such a rich blessing and full experience that you don't even miss it. The greater love, the greater joy, the greater excitement that you have in serving the Lord far exceeds the ungodly things that used to turn you on. You feel captivated and thrilled with the beauty of this new relationship you have with God. The music of Jesus in your heart is so much richer. This life in Christ is so much better than the old stuff, and soon you lose the desire for sinful things. God works from within to pour into you His love and His grace.

Love, Then Service

Do you realize the importance Jesus puts upon your loving Him? He accepts only the works that flow from a heart of love. He's not at all interested in the works you might do out of a sense of obligation or responsibility. He wants your service to Him to flow out of a heart of love. It must be the overflow of love and the expression of your love for Him.

I've heard people complain about the things they "have to do" for the Lord. "Oh, I suppose I have to visit Brother So-and-so," they grumble. How sad that a believer would try to serve God out of a grumbling sense of duty rather than the fulfillment of love. Too many of us speak of heavy burdens that we must carry.

But Jesus said, "My yoke is easy and My burden is light" (Matthew 11:30). So if you discover that the burden you're trying to carry is so heavy that it weighs you down, then you had better take a second look at that burden. It probably isn't from Him. It may be something that you've taken upon yourself or allowed others to lay on you—and that can be a heavy burden.

People try to lay their burdens on me all the time. Someone messes up his life and then comes to me and says, "Fix it, Chuck. It's your problem." No, it is not my problem; it's his problem. "Don't lay your burden on me," I say. "The Bible says, 'Casting all your care upon Him, for He cares for you'" (1 Peter 5:7). If you try to take responsibility for lifting someone out of a hole that he's dug for himself, that can be a terribly heavy burden.

Don't try to serve God out of a begrudging sense of duty. Remember that one day your works will be judged—and the only kind of works that God will accept are those motivated by love. Paul the apostle said, "For the love of Christ compels us" (2 Corinthians 5:14). The compelling love of Jesus Christ within works in such a way that we no longer look upon our service as a sacrifice. We look upon it as a privilege, as a joy, as a blessing. What fun to be able to do things for our Lord who loves us so much.

The Lord does not long for our service; He longs for a growing, loving relationship with us. God simply wants a loving relationship with you.

So don't try to substitute your works for the fellowship He desires! Rather than busying yourself for Him, He would rather that you just sit, relax, and share time and love with Him. *Serving the Lord always follows loving the Lord.* You serve the Lord because you love Him; that is the mark of the bondslave.

In ancient times, a man who desired to remain the property of his master would say, "I love my master. I don't want to be free of him. I want to serve him." The master would then take the servant to the doorpost and pin him with an awl through the lobe of his ear. Ever after, that servant would remain the master's bondslave.

"I love my Master. That's why I want to serve Him." This is the only true motive for any valued service to God. You must have this motivation for whatever you do for Him. It is the only motivation the Lord will accept.

A Heart of Joy

Several hundred years ago a saint named Teresa of Avila used to say a prayer that I think still has some legs. "From silly devotions and sour-faced saints," she prayed, "spare us, O Lord." I believe that a sour-faced Christian is probably one of the poorest witnesses in the world.

During one tragic period of church history—and there have been many—believers had the idea that smiling made you suspect. Laughing was an outright sin. It was taught that Christians should be very sober and somber and never display a jovial spirit. Believers practiced a stained-glass voice, folded their hands, bent their necks and with a sorrowful look said, "Brother, I shall pray for you." They thought the more solemn you appeared, the more spiritual you were. There was no joy, no laughter, no excitement regarding the things of the Lord. They considered a somber look a mark of deep spirituality.

It was a terrible witness.

"But let all those rejoice who put their trust in You," the Bible says by contrast. "Let them ever shout for joy, because You defend them; let those also who love Your name be joyful in You" (Psalm 5:11). The Bible describes the Christian life as one of delighted joy: "For the kingdom of God is not eating and drinking, but righteousness and peace and joy in the Holy Spirit" (Romans 14:17).

So enjoy your walk with God! The strongest witness you can have is the joy of the Lord, even in the middle of the most difficult situations. Remember the old song, "I've got the joy, joy, joy, joy down in my heart." We used to add a verse to it, "I've got the happy hope that heckles heathens down in my heart." Such joy really can bother some people.

Imagine you're facing bankruptcy. Someone is bound to say to you, "I hear what you're going through, brother. I feel so bad for you." What would happen if you responded, "You know, the Lord is so good; I just love the Lord! I know He'll take care of it, one way or another"?

He'll look at you with furrowed brow and say, "Man, don't you understand what's happening? Don't you know that you're broke? What are you going to do about all your bills?"

When you remain happy with the joy of the Lord in such miserable conditions, you heckle the heathens. They just cannot handle it. But it is a real witness.

Singing in a Prison

One day Paul and his ministry buddy, Silas, got thrown into a filthy prison for freeing a slave girl from demon possession. The local magistrates ordered them beaten and placed in stocks in the inner dungeon, a place full of rats, disease, and all kinds of filth. Nobody had washed off their dried blood, and now it was caked on their raw backs. In fact, no one did anything to help them. They simply left them in this miserable condition.

Paul and Silas were in a strange land, behind bars without any hope of release. They didn't know how long they would be in prison. Their backs still smarted from the beating they had endured, and things looked desperate.

Imagine if you were thrown in a Tijuana jail, with no one to bail you out. No one knows where you are; they know only that you went on a ministry trip to Mexico. They have no idea why you haven't returned. No doubt you'd be wondering, *What's going to happen to me? How long will I be here in this miserable place?* And you'd probably ask, *Why, God, would You allow this to happen? Lord, did You really call us to Mexico? Did we make a mistake in thinking You were calling us down here?* Questions would fly through your mind. *How will we ever get released from here? When will You get us out of this mess?* How do you suppose you would react if you found yourself in such miserable conditions?

Paul and Silas reacted by singing praises to the Lord.

Sitting in those painful stocks, the two men prayed and sang praises. The other prisoners heard them—and you can well imagine the crude remarks they employed to tell Paul and Silas to just shut up. But at midnight the bars began to shake when a strong earthquake rumbled the very foundations of the prison. All the cell doors burst open, awakening the guard. Figuring that the prisoners had all escaped—and fearing his inevitable and severe punishment—the guard took out his sword to commit suicide.

"Don't do harm to yourself!" Paul called out. "We are all here."

In the darkness the guard sought out Paul and Silas, and in a trembling voice said, "Sirs, what must I do to be saved?"

When we find ourselves in difficult, confusing circumstances, what a great opportunity we have to pray and to praise the Lord! You might not be able to praise God for your circumstances, but you can praise Him. Because even though your feet are locked in the stocks, your spirit is free. Rather than feeling sorry for yourself because of your physical misery, you can sing praises to your Lord.

That takes a transformed heart!

As you pray and sing, you will find your faith growing and your worries fleeing. Soon you can find yourself rejoicing in the goodness of God, in the greatness of His power and the immensity of His love, knowing He's in control and He will not fail.

Jesus Never Fails

As a young boy my brother had serious asthma attacks. Whenever he would get one, my mother would come into the room, lift him out of bed and carry him into another room.

That room had an old rocking chair that squeaked whenever someone used it. My mother would rock him in that chair, and as I would lay there in bed, I could hear him wheezing and fighting for breath. I could also hear my mother singing: "Jesus never fails, Jesus never fails. Heaven and earth shall pass away, but Jesus never fails."[4] That song became her anthem.

As my three siblings and I grew up, we often required Mom's help. She would pray and she would sing, "Jesus never fails, Jesus never fails. Heaven and earth shall pass away, but Jesus never fails." It became so much her life theme that when she died, we had those words inscribed on her tombstone. If you were to visit my mother's grave at Fairhaven Cemetery, you would see the words, "Jesus never fails."

And He hasn't yet, and He won't.

The really interesting thing is that not long ago I was in Santa Barbara, presiding over a memorial service for a relative. My mother's mother had been buried at that cemetery. So we asked at the office where we

4 *Jesus Never Fails,* words and music by Arthur A. Luther, © 1927 by Singspiration Music.

could find my grandmother's burial place. They showed us its location on a map and after the service we went looking for my grandmother's grave. I had never been there before, so you can imagine my surprise when we found it and I read her tombstone: "Jesus never fails."

What a marvelous testimony to pass down from generation to generation. You can put that on my tombstone when I go: "Jesus never fails."

You may be going through some hardships. There may be some difficult things that you just don't understand—the "whys" of whatever is happening to you. But know this: He loves you, He's concerned, He knows all about it, He's in control, and He will not fail. That conviction, more than anything, will transform you into a follower of Christ whose heart beats wholly for Him.

PART THREE

God's Love Through Us to Others

"And this commandment we have from Him: that he who loves God must love his brother also."

1 JOHN 4:21

The heart of the Christian gospel is love—God loving you, you loving God supremely, and you loving your neighbor as yourself. That's the heart and the essence of the Christian message.

Our heavenly Father calls you and me to so love Him and one another that we might clearly demonstrate what true Christianity is all about. Never has the world more desperately needed such a demonstration. What too often passes itself off as Christianity today is only another form of hollow religion, woefully lacking in love. God calls us to love as He loves—and that's not something we can conjure up within ourselves. It will happen only as we ask Him to plant His love in our hearts. Only then will we love as He loves.

Love Commanded

ANYONE WHO ASKS JESUS a question—especially a loaded one—should prepare to get more of an answer than he bargained for.

A lot more.

One afternoon Jesus' opponents sought to get Him in hot water with the Roman authorities. So they asked Him whether a pious Jew should pay taxes to Caesar. When Jesus' answer dumbfounded them, other challengers in the crowd asked a question they considered much tougher. And when His brilliant answer silenced them, still other skittish observers said, "Teacher, You have spoken well." At that point Luke adds—I'm guessing with a twinkle in his eye—"after that they dared not question Him anymore" (Luke 20:39-40).

As I said, when you ask Jesus a question, get prepared for a surprising answer!

That certainly happened the day a lawyer asked Him to name "the first commandment." Without hesitation, Jesus gave the expected answer:

> The first of all the commandments is: "Hear, O Israel, the Lord our God, the Lord is one. And you shall love the Lord your God with all your heart, with all your soul, with all your mind, and with all your strength." This is the first commandment (Mark 12:29-30).

So far, so good. I'm sure a lot of heads in the audience nodded in approval. But then came the "more-than-you-bargained-for" part.

> And the second, like it, is this: "You shall love your neighbor as yourself." There is no other commandment greater than these (Mark 12:31).

A *second* commandment like the first? Nobody had asked Jesus about this! Still, He gave it to them anyway. And then to top things off, He made it clear that these two commandments were really just different sides of the same, single commandment. "There is no other commandment"—singular—"greater than these," Jesus insisted.

Jesus immediately tied love of one's neighbor to love for God. The two actions are inseparable. Love for God has to come first, but love for neighbors must follow. You cannot love God without subsequently loving your neighbor, and you cannot love your neighbor without first loving God.

The Rich Young Ruler

A wealthy young man we usually remember as "the rich young ruler" once came to Jesus and knelt at His feet. "Good Teacher," he said, "what shall I do that I may inherit eternal life?"

"Why do you call Me good?" Jesus replied. "No one is good but One, that is, God. You know the commandments: 'Do not commit adultery,'

'Do not murder,' 'Do not steal,' 'Do not bear false witness,' 'Do not defraud,' 'Honor your father and your mother.'"

"Teacher," the man answered, "all these things I have kept from my youth."

Mark tells us that Jesus looked at the man and loved him, and said, "One thing you lack: go your way, sell whatever you have and give to the poor, and you will have treasure in heaven; and come, take up the cross, and follow Me" (Mark 10:17-21).

And once again, a stunned man got more of an answer from Jesus than he had anticipated. When this young man heard Jesus' answer, his face fell, he turned around and he began to slowly walk away, great sorrow filling his heart—and all because he could not let go of his great wealth.

The really amazing thing here is that, apparently, he could tell Jesus with a straight face, "Lord, I have kept all these commandments from the time I was a boy. You know, I haven't stolen. I haven't committed adultery. I haven't lied to anyone about my neighbors." Great! Jesus didn't challenge him on any of those claims. But He did want the man to get to the real heart of God's law, which comes down to loving God supremely and loving your neighbor as yourself.

Wouldn't it seem that if such a rich man loved his neighbor as himself, he would have busied himself with helping some of his less fortunate neighbors? After all, he had said, "I have kept all of God's commandments from my youth."

Unfortunately, most of us have a view of ourselves that differs significantly from God's. We're prone to overlook our flaws and our faults. We justify ourselves. We give good reasons for why we react as we do.

But are they valid in God's eyes?

Notice that in His answer, Jesus mentioned nothing of the first table of the law. He did not bring up the man's relationship to God. Jesus did not quote any of the first four commandments: "You shall have no other gods before Me," "You shall not make for yourself a carved image," "You shall not take the name of the Lord your God in vain," "Remember the Sabbath day, to keep it holy" (Exodus 20:3-8). He dealt only with man's relationship with other men and women. Why? Because this man was a moralist.

I see the rich young ruler as a typical man, looking to do some good work in order to earn eternal life. He was *used* to doing good works. Apparently, he spent his life doing good works. And so Jesus focused his attention on his relationship with his fellow men—and when the man realized how much it would cost him to love his neighbor as he loved himself, he left brokenhearted.

The rich young ruler had come to Jesus quite sure of his love for God. He left Jesus, clinging more to his money than to a commitment to love his neighbors as he loved himself.

You Already Love Yourself

When Jesus commands us to love our neighbors as we love ourselves, He isn't saying (as many insist these days), "You have to learn to love yourself first." No, He's simply acknowledging that we already do love ourselves. We don't have to work on that; it's inborn.

Developing self-esteem is not the greatest need of humankind today. Nor is the lack of self-esteem the greatest sin in the world. The greatest sin in the world is the rejection of Jesus Christ, and the world's greatest need is submitting to Jesus Christ.

Every one of us, without exception, loves ourselves. So the Bible says, "For no one ever hated his own flesh, but nourishes and cherishes it, just as the Lord does the church" (Ephesians 5:29).

"You're wrong, Chuck," someone says. "I hate myself! I really do. I look in the mirror and I'm so ugly, I just hate myself."

Wait a minute! This person in the mirror that you say you hate, are you angry because he or she is ugly? Or are you happy because you see such ugliness in your reflection? If you *really* hated yourself, then you'd say, "Man, that person is so ugly, I just *love* it! Ha, ha, ha, I'm so ugly. How great! Because I hate me."

But you don't do that, do you? Of course not. No one does. Why not? Because we all want the best for ourselves—and that's what love is, wanting the best for someone. Blaise Pascal, the French mathematician and philosopher, used to say that even those who hanged themselves demonstrated their self-love, because in taking their own lives, they hoped to improve their difficult situation.

Or think of it in another way. If I were to videotape the congregation coming out of church this week, and then later I were to put up a big screen to show the video, who would you be looking for on the screen?

"Shhhh! Quiet! *I'm next.*"

Maybe I'm different from everyone else, but when I look at a group picture, I always look first for *me*. I want to see how I look. I want to see if I closed my eyes when the flash went off—and if I did, then it's a horrible picture. It's an ugly photo. Tear it up! Even though everyone else may look great, if I look bad, it's a horrible picture and should be destroyed.

You love yourself enough to see that you get three square meals a day; don't you?

You love yourself enough to see that you have opportunities for a little luxury once in a while; don't you?

You love yourself enough to see that you have a roof over your head; don't you?

You love yourself enough to see that you're comfortable; don't you?

The Lord doesn't command you to love yourself. He knows He doesn't have to, because you do that automatically. That's why I refuse to believe the idea that you have to learn to love yourself in order to love your neighbor. That's a bunch of baloney. *We all love ourselves*. This foolishness that, "You have to learn to love yourself so you can love your neighbor" is not scriptural. The Lord recognizes that we already do love ourselves. Certainly that love, like everything else, got twisted in the fall when Adam and Eve disobeyed God in the garden; but it's still there.

So when Jesus says, "Love your neighbor as you love yourself," He means, "just as you naturally want the best for yourself, so you must want the best for your neighbor."

Do you think that sounds easy? It's not.

Love Your Neighbor

It's tough to love my neighbor as I love myself. While I naturally want the best for myself, to love my neighbor *as myself* takes the help and the grace of God. It doesn't come naturally. In fact, to demonstrate how *un*natural it is, ask yourself one simple question:

Am I as concerned with my neighbor's need as I am with my own need?

And if you answered, "Yes!" you're lying.

The only way to develop this kind of love for your neighbor—God's kind of love—is to ask God to put it in your heart. You don't naturally have this kind of love, any more than I do. But we really can become conduits of God's love. We really can allow His love to flow through us to others.

The moment God moves to the center of your life—as soon as you bow to the Lord and submit your life to God as King—you become a conduit to spread His love to others. Through Him you can love your neighbor as yourself. But unless God is at the center of your life, you will never be able to do so.

And God's love, of course, will work no ill to its neighbor. If you love someone, you're not going to lie to him, steal from him, or cheat him in any way—especially if you love him as you love yourself.

So Jesus' command to love our neighbors as ourselves strikes at the heart of the self-centered life. You cannot fulfill His command unless you first love God supremely. Only as you love God supremely can you fulfill the second part of the Great Commandment, which is loving your neighbor as much as you love yourself. A loving relationship with God provides the power for you to have meaningful and lasting relationships with your fellow man.

You and I need God at the vertical axis of our lives in order to balance our relationships on the horizontal plane. And if we don't balance our relationships on the horizontal plane—that is, if we don't love our neighbor as we love ourselves—then Jesus would call our professed love for God nothing but a sham.

Messed Up on the Horizontal Plane

I don't have to tell you that people get all messed up on this horizontal plane. We seem to have an almost endless supply of methods and tactics to totally mess up our relationships.

To deal with this problem, many of us get an appointment with a shrink. We want him to help us understand ourselves. "Why do I react like this? Why do I respond like that? Why do I yell? Why do I scream? Why do I drive people away? Why do I act in such an anti-social manner?"

And the shrink tries to delve into our psyches in order to tell us, "Now, if you'll just do this and that, and take this little pill I'll prescribe for you, then things should improve eventually." He does the best he can to help us balance out our interpersonal relationships that have gone so badly haywire on the horizontal plane.

But no sooner do we get one relationship in focus and bring some balance to it, than five other relationships slide to the other side of the ship—and before we know it, the whole vessel begins to take on water. We watch one side sink while the other side goes way up, so we sprint over to the high side to balance the thing out—and we spend our whole lives trying to keep things in balance.

But it always remains topsy-turvy to one degree or another.

The only permanent solution is to come back to the center axis. Bad human relationships indicate that our relationship with God is way off track. If our axis is tilted, then the horizontal plane spinning around that axis will continue to fly about in a crazy whirl. And it'll continue to move up and down, round and round, until we say, "Oh God, stop this thing! I want off!"

We must learn to keep first things first. The first is to know God, get right with God, and love God. When we focus on that, then the second will begin to fall into order. Only then will we find the ability to love our neighbor as we love ourselves.

From Negative to Positive

Let's return to the Ten Commandments for a moment. The first four commandments concern our relationship to God. He communicated them to us primarily in the negative: "You shall not, you shall not, you shall not."

Jesus takes these same commandments and shifts them to the positive: "You shall love the Lord your God, completely and totally." That takes care of the negatives. If you have a positive love for God, then you don't have to worry much about the negatives.

The last six commandments have to do with your relationship with your fellow man: "Honor your father and your mother," "You shall not commit adultery," "You shall not murder," "You shall not steal," "You shall not lie," "You shall not covet" (Exodus 20:12-17). Once again, most get stated in the negative: "You shall not."

And once more, Jesus summarizes them with a positive: "Love your neighbor as you already love yourself." That single positive command, again, takes care of all the negatives. When you love your neighbor as yourself, you don't have to worry about violating some prohibition against harming someone. Your love will act like a guardrail against sin and selfishness.

Loving God foremost fulfills every law that deals with your relationship with the Lord, while loving your neighbor as yourself fulfills every obligation to your fellow man. Simple enough; isn't it?

And yet, in our natural states, we don't much care for the sound of this. It seems pretty daunting! So we step into the sandals of the lawyer who didn't appreciate Jesus' answer about the Great Commandment. Along with him we ask, "And just who is my neighbor?"

And once again, Jesus gives us a little more than we bargained for.

Who Is My Neighbor?

As He often did, Jesus responded to this question with a memorable story. Since we seem to get the point of stories better than we sometimes grasp abstract concepts, Jesus offered a tale with some familiar characters: a Jewish businessman, a pair of religious professionals, and a Samaritan—a hated half-breed despised by most of Jesus' contemporaries.

To fully appreciate the story, we should remind ourselves of a little history. When Assyria invaded and destroyed the northern kingdom of Israel—often called Samaria, after its capital city—hundreds of years before Jesus' day, the conquerors deported most of the Hebrew population. The Assyrians replaced the Israelites with foreigners, who intermarried with the few Hebrews left behind. Soon this mixed race had corrupted the Old Testament religious practices of the whole region. More than two centuries later, when streams of freed Jewish people returned to their homeland after the Babylonian captivity, these Samaritans still lived in the north—and the two groups did *not* get along.

So Jesus told a story about a Jewish businessman who took a trip from Jerusalem to Jericho. Along the way a band of robbers surprised him, beat him up and took all his belongings, leaving him for dead. As he lay bleeding on the side of the road, a priest came by and saw the man in his desperate need—but he pulled his robes tight around him and made his way past the moaning victim. Soon afterwards, a Levite, another religious professional came by. He also ignored the beaten man and hurried on his way.

But then a Samaritan came riding past the same spot. When he saw the injured man, whom he instantly recognized as Jewish, he got down off his donkey and cleaned the man's wounds. He placed the man's injured body on his own animal and stopped at an inn halfway between Jerusalem and Jericho. There he said to the innkeeper, "I have to continue my journey, but take care of this man. Whatever expenses you incur, when I return, I'll take care of them. Bill it to me."

When Jesus finished His story, he turned to the lawyer who had asked the question and said, "Which of these men acted as a neighbor to the fellow in need?" The lawyer got the point instantly.

Who is my neighbor? Whoever is in need.

It's worth noting that Jesus made an outsider the hero of His story, as He did so often. In all of their self-righteousness, the priest and the Levite did nothing to help their wounded countryman. They boasted of a close relationship with God, yet their actions denied their claims.

As Paul would write many years later, "They profess to know God, but in works they deny Him" (Titus 1:16). And who was the one character in Jesus' story who chose to help the dying man? A hated Samaritan. He becomes the hero of the story. The one character sure to raise some hackles is the one Jesus lifts up to the starring role.

Again, more answer than anyone bargained for!

If we're walking in the love of Jesus Christ, we will reach out to whomever might have a need. Who is a "Samaritan" to you? What class of person or sort of individual makes you uncomfortable? His or her need should touch your heart because it touches the heart of God.

Remember how Jesus described His Father? He said that we serve a loving God who takes special note even when a little sparrow falls to the ground (Matthew 10:29). As His emissaries and representatives on earth, we therefore must allow ourselves to be moved by the needs of our countrymen and the "Samaritans" who live among us. We all live in the world created by our heavenly Father, and He expects us to show love to anyone who lives on this planet.

So Jesus said, "Love your neighbor as yourself." And who is my neighbor? Whoever has a need.

To Sum Up

Matthew's gospel tells us that after Jesus answered the lawyer's question, He said, "On these two commandments hang all the Law and the Prophets" (Matthew 22:40). That's quite a summary statement!

He meant that when you love God supremely and when you love your neighbor as yourself, you have mastered the fundamental teaching of the entire Old Testament. That's the heart of the Bible's message from Genesis to Malachi! All of the Law and all of the Prophets "hang" on loving God with everything you have and on loving your neighbor with the same kind of concern that you naturally show to yourself.

If you live like this, you won't *need* the "*You shall not steal,*" "*You shall not lie,*" "*You shall not commit adultery.*" You simply don't require the laws to tell you how to live to please God. The first table of the law (the first four commandments) is summed up in loving God supremely, while the second table of the law (the last six commandments) is summed up in loving your neighbor as yourself. If you get that, then you've got it all. The Ten Commandments are all covered right there. If you do these two things, then you have fulfilled God's commandments.

Paul the apostle certainly understood this, for he wrote,

> For the commandments, You shall not commit adultery, You shall not murder, You shall not steal, You shall not bear false witness, You shall not covet, and if there is any other commandment, are all summed up in this saying, namely, You shall love your neighbor as yourself (Romans 13:9).

Everything that God has commanded us about how we ought to live in relationship to God and in relationship to each other is summed up in these two instructions: love God supremely, and love your neighbor as you love yourself. If you do this, you will be doing all that God requires of you. When you love in this way, you fulfill God's law. Paul said it like this:

> For all the law is fulfilled in one word, even in this: "You shall love your neighbor as yourself" (Galatians 5:14).

As you walk in the Spirit, you will be walking in love—and then there doesn't need to be a law to regulate your life. Laws, you see, are for unprincipled people. Those who live by godly principles don't require laws that prohibit evil behavior. Such laws are necessary to restrain unprincipled people. But if you're walking in love—supreme love for God and supreme love for your fellow man—then no law is necessary. For you, all of the law is fulfilled.

This is what the whole Old Testament proclaimed. The Law and the Prophets—and every holy book in between—hang on these two commands:

You shall love the L*ORD your God with all your heart, with all your soul, with all your mind, and with all your strength.*

AND

You shall love your neighbor as yourself.

You cannot find any greater instruction anywhere in the Old Testament. This is the pinnacle. This is the summit. This is the apex.

Do Well!

Paul was not the only New Testament writer to understand that the Great Commandment represents the whole driving force of the entire Old Testament. An apostle whom some people like to pit against the apostle Paul came to the same conclusion, even though he didn't call it "the Great Commandment." James wrote,

> If you really fulfill the royal law according to the Scripture, "You shall love your neighbor as yourself," you do well (James 2:8).

James called it "the royal law." Remember, this is the same man who just a little earlier in his letter wrote, "Be doers of the Word and not hearers only, deceiving yourself" (James 1:22).

And what does it mean for you and me to be "doers" of the Word? In essence, we must love our neighbor as ourselves—and James makes it clear that real love is not manifested primarily by the words we speak. It's not like Lucy in the old *Peanuts* cartoon, who said, "I love the world. It's people I hate." No, genuine love manifests itself in genuinely loving actions.

And really, isn't that where the rich young ruler failed? He wanted to know how he could inherit eternal life—something that should concern all of us—and he thought he had been doing pretty well.

He felt sure he had been keeping the law. Still, something ate at him inside. He knew *something* wasn't right in his life. He intuitively knew that he hadn't yet achieved eternal life, but he couldn't put his finger on the particular reason why. So he asked Jesus to help him identify what he lacked.

Jesus didn't tell the young man to love God more; He told him to love his neighbors as he already loved himself. He said, in essence, "Son, it's time for you to use some of that wealth of yours to keep the royal law. Love your neighbor as yourself!"

But it's easy to say and hard to do; isn't it? Especially when your neighbor doesn't love you back. You might be able to love your neighbor as yourself when he says, "Why, what a great guy you are! I just *love* living next door to you!" But how about when he says, "How did I wind up with a rotten neighbor as stupid and oafish as you?" That's quite a different assignment; isn't it?

And yet James says to us, "If you really fulfill the royal law according to the Scripture, 'You shall love your neighbor as yourself,' you do well."

How about you? Are *you* doing well? It's what the whole Old Testament is all about.

Love Described

GOD WANTED A WORD to describe how we ought to "love" others, and He chose the same Greek term, *agape*, that He used to describe His own love. We are to love others just as God loves us!

So what does it mean, exactly, to love others as God loves us? Fortunately, the apostle Paul did us a huge favor in 1 Corinthians 13 when he very carefully described the kind of love God calls us to demonstrate.

Throughout his famous "Love Chapter," Paul used the Greek term *agape* to draw a clear and compelling picture of the kind of love that God expects to flow out of His children. Let's take a short tour through the last ten verses of that amazing chapter to glimpse a few highlights of the *agape* love God wants to pour through us to others.

Paul says that love:

... suffers long

The idea here is that *agape* keeps putting up with repeated provocations. Most of us have some number that serves as our outer limit; often that number is three. "Okay, that's the third time you've done that," we say, "and *now* I've had it!"

Peter selected his own number. One day when he thought of himself as really growing in grace—certainly far more than his fellow disciples—he said to Jesus, "Lord, how often should I forgive a brother for the same offense?" Then he mentally doubled our three and added one for good measure: "Seven times?"

Peter clearly expected the Lord to say, "Wow, Peter, you are *really* growing! Seven times? That is *great.*" But that isn't what Jesus told Peter. Instead He replied, "Peter, don't forgive him seven times, but seventy times seven" (Matthew 18:22).

Peter must have thought, *Are you kidding me? That's four hundred and ninety times!*

So what did Jesus mean? Longsuffering is not a matter of mathematics, but a matter of spirit. It is an attitude that doesn't keep track of offenses. So I don't keep a running account and say, "478 ... 479 ..." until you reach seventy times seven—and then *kapow*, you get it. Clearly, Jesus figured that Peter would lose count by the time he got to 490 and would realize that longsuffering is a matter of spirit and not mathematics.

Agape love puts up, and puts up past counting. It is longsuffering.

... and is kind;

At the end of a long period of longsuffering, *agape* love remains kind. It doesn't seek retribution and vengeance. I have heard people say, "I've put up with that irritating behavior long enough. *Now* he's going to wish he hadn't crossed me!" That's anything but kind. That isn't *agape*. The kind of love God wants to pour through you to others says, "Yes, I have taken, and taken, and taken some more—that poor soul. God help him!" *Agape* love is kind even after it suffers long.

... does not envy;

Agape love is so great that it rejoices in the blessings of others. It doesn't feel envious of what someone else has received. It doesn't get jealous of what others have gained. Instead it says, "Because I love you, I rejoice in the good things that have happened to you. I rejoice that your number got picked instead of mine. I rejoice that you received the promotion. I rejoice, because I love you."

... does not parade itself,

We live in a world of constant hype. It seems that nearly everything today is a big marketing promotion for this, or a huge endorsement for that. Unfortunately, this kind of hype has crept into the church, so we see churches trying to promote their programs—or worse, pastors trying to promote themselves.

But *agape* love doesn't seek to promote itself. It doesn't go around boasting of how loving it is. What did Shakespeare say? "Methinks thou dost protest too much." I always get a little concerned when people repeatedly tell me how much they love me. Sometimes I feel like Shakespeare, "You're laying it on a little thick, brother." I tend to get leery of these constant assurances, because I've been burned by those who professed their tremendous love and devotion to me using flowery and overly flattering verbiage. *Agape* love doesn't parade itself. It doesn't brag about its strength or its ardor. It doesn't have to.

... is not puffed up;

Agape love doesn't have a superior attitude. It doesn't view itself as better than others. It doesn't look down on people. It doesn't create class distinctions. The Bible says that while love builds up, it isn't puffed up.

... does not behave rudely,

The *King James Version* translates this phrase, "doth not behave itself unseemly." In other words, it isn't weird.

Years ago in my school years, we had a gal in our class who flipped out while studying opera. She had really developed her voice and had learned to project it. You could hear her for five city blocks around. But she had become weird, to put it graciously.

She dressed weird, believing it to be godly. She always pulled her hair straight back and in a bun, because that was godly. She never wore any makeup, because that was ungodly. She had all of these little ideas of what constituted righteousness and holiness and godliness.

I worked in downtown Los Angeles and used to ride the streetcar back to my dorm after work. Evidently she worked downtown, too. Sometimes she would get on the same streetcar I had boarded. As soon as she spotted me, she would use that loud, operatic voice to say, "PRAISE THE LORD, BROTHER!" Her voice reverberated through the whole streetcar, drawing immediate attention to this weird-looking gal.

I found it all terribly embarrassing. Who wanted to be identified with somebody weird like that? Everyone's head in the car would turn to see the intended recipient of her greeting—mine included.

So after a while, whenever I saw her waiting for my streetcar, I scampered out the back door before she could come through the front door. I'd then wait and take the next car home—*well* worth the extra dime.

Agape love doesn't behave rudely or in an unseemly manner. It doesn't make a spectacle of itself. It doesn't try to attract undue attention.

... *does not seek its own,*

Agape love defers to others. It doesn't insist on its own way. It never says, "If you don't let me be captain, I'm going to go home and I won't play with you anymore." It simply doesn't seek its own way, since it wants what's best for others.

... *is not provoked,*

In the *King James Version* you will see "is not *easily* provoked." Unfortunately, the word "easily" does not appear in any of the Greek manuscripts. I say "unfortunately," because I used to say, "Well, I am *not* easily provoked. If you work hard at it, you can upset me, but not easily."

Then I started looking through the original Greek text of this passage, and I discovered that it doesn't appear in any ancient manuscript. The text actually says, "is not provoked," without the "easily."

So how did the "easily" get in there? The classic commentator Adam Clarke (1762-1832) solves the mystery: "The translation made and printed by the command of King James ... improperly inserts the word 'easily,' which might have been his majesty's own [instruction] ... our own authorized version is the only one which I have seen where this false reading appears."

Whether the idea came from King James or from one of his translators, someone apparently thought, *Not provoked at all? That is too heavy. Who isn't provoked at some time or another?* So at the king's command, the word "easily" got inserted into the text; but to be true to the Word, we have to take it out. *Agape* love just "is not provoked," period.

... *thinks no evil;*

This kind of love is guileless, without suspicion. It doesn't look for hidden motives. It doesn't search for a secret agenda.

A woman from a church I once pastored frequently came up to me moments after I had greeted her to say, "Now, when you said 'hello,' what did you *really* mean?" I meant "hello!" But she would always take some phrase and ask, conspiratorially, "What did you *really* mean by that?" She was always looking for some subtle, hidden meaning. Listen, I'm not smart enough to speak in subtleties. I have little choice but to say what I mean and mean what I say.

Agape love doesn't think evil of anyone. It thinks the best, until evidence proves otherwise. And even then, it still refuses to think evil.

... does not rejoice in iniquity,

When someone who has been causing you a lot of problems suddenly wrecks his brand new car, how do you feel? "At last! He got what was coming to him. He deserved that, and I've waited a long time to see it happen." That isn't *agape* love. God's love doesn't rejoice when an enemy gets put down, wiped out or throttled. *Agape* love doesn't rejoice in iniquity.

... but rejoices in the truth;

Agape love doesn't fear the truth; it rejoices in it. The declaration of truth—whatever that truth is—gives it occasion to exult.

... bears all things,

Insults. Hardship. Persecution. Slander. Misfortune. Disaster. *Agape* love bears up under them all, enduring, persevering, and overcoming.

... believes all things,

Agape love doesn't require you to believe in Santa Claus and the Easter Bunny just as you believe in the resurrection of Christ. *Agape* love puts no stock in such myths and fantasies, but it does believe every word that proceeds from the mouth of God. It stands on His promises, regardless of how things may look. *Agape* love believes that God never fails. And it certainly believes that He *never* abandons those He loves.

... *hopes all things,*

Christianity is a forward-looking faith. It expects the best. Since it looks to God, it knows that "every good gift and every perfect gift is from above, and comes down from the Father of lights, with whom there is no variation or shadow of turning" (James 1:17). Since it trusts in an almighty, loving God, *agape* love has an unquenchable positive outlook.

... *endures all things.*

Yet despite its positive outlook, *agape* knows where it lives—on a planet infected with sin, in terrible rebellion against God. Therefore, this kind of love expects some difficulties along with the triumphs. It recognizes that endurance has a vital and honored place in its relational toolbox. And it looks heavenward for the strength to persevere, no matter what.

... *Love never fails.*

Without question, many good things shall fail. The gifts of the Spirit, for example, shall one day cease. They are for now. We need them now. They are important to us now—but one day these gifts will all pass away. Why? Because we will no longer need them. Paul highlights that which is transient and temporal in order to compare it with that which is lasting and enduring.

... *But whether there are prophecies, they will fail;*

In heaven I will have to seek another occupation, for when we are with Jesus, whom will there be to exhort, to edify, or to comfort? We will already have everything we need. I won't have to exhort anyone to seek the Lord or to commit themselves to Him, for we will all be right there with Him. I won't have to comfort anyone; all of our trials will have ended. We will bask forever in the glory of His presence.

And so this gift of prophecy has a limited time value. It is good now; it is needed now. But the time will soon come when prophecy will fail. Once the Lord returns, it will no longer be necessary.

... whether there are tongues, they will cease;

This refers to the gift of speaking in an unknown tongue, the *glossolalia*, given by the Holy Spirit to assist us in communicating the deep things of our spirits to God. It is designed to help us in our worship and to assist us in our praise. But in heaven we will be in His very presence, so tongues will no longer be necessary. And thus, this gift of tongues will cease as well.

... whether there is knowledge, it will vanish away.

This refers to the word of knowledge, in which God gives us specific knowledge or insight to help us in dealing with a particular situation. This gift never gives us more than partial knowledge. We never receive total and complete information regarding a situation, but only enough to help us deal with it and so give glory to God.

In heaven, however, what purpose would such a gift serve? As Paul is about to tell us, when we see Jesus face to face, we will know Him even as we are known. So what information could we lack that a word of knowledge would supply?

... For we know in part and we prophesy in part.

Prophecy, tongues, and the word of knowledge will all one day pass off the scene. Prophecies will fail. Tongues will cease. Knowledge will vanish away. For these things are all just partial. We know in part; we prophesy in part,

... But when that which is perfect has come, then that which is in part will be done away.

Controversy arose in the past hundred years over the phrase, "that which is perfect." While every Bible commentator prior to the twentieth century understood it to refer to the second coming of Jesus Christ, that all changed after 1906. That's when a modern charismatic movement, eventually called Pentecostalism, reignited an interest in the gifts of the Spirit.

Certain fundamentalist preachers who wanted to discount this movement turned to 1 Corinthians 13 and brought out a new interpretation of "that which is perfect." No longer did it refer to the return of Jesus Christ, as the church had always maintained through nineteen long centuries. Now, they said, it referred to the full revelation of the Word of God. In their view, once the church received the whole canon of Scripture, we no longer needed the supernatural gifts of prophecy, tongues, and the word of knowledge. When "that which is perfect"—the Bible—had come by the end of the apostolic age, all those spiritual gifts ceased.

Yet such an interpretation cannot stand. As G. Campbell Morgan pointed out, the text very clearly says we will see Jesus "face to face" when "that which is perfect" has come. Have you seen Jesus face to face? Neither have I. Paul also says that on that day we will "know Him even as we are known." Now, Jesus knows us perfectly; but do you know Him perfectly at this moment? Neither do I. So rather than being proof against the exercise of the gifts of prophecy or tongues or word of knowledge, in reality, this portion of Scripture is a wonderful support, because it makes clear that these gifts are given to us until Jesus returns in power and glory—"that which is perfect."

> ... *When I was a child, I spoke as a child, I understood as a child, I thought as a child; but when I became a man, I put away childish things.*

When I stand in the presence of my Lord, I will be complete. Many of the things I do today will appear very childish as I look back on them as a glorified believer. Yet I won't come into that completeness and fullness until I am with the Lord.

> ... *For now we see in a mirror, dimly,*

The craftsmen of Paul's day had not yet perfected the process of making mirrors. Not until the thirteenth century or so did artisans learn how to create modern mirrors using glass with a silver backing. Prior to that time, mirrors were nothing but highly polished metal, making a true reflection nearly impossible. Quite often the reflection looked distorted, hazy, dim. Paul says that until the Lord returns, we will see Jesus and His truth dimly, as in a distorted metal mirror.

... but then face to face.

When the Lord comes again, we will at last understand completely. At that point we will see everything with absolute clarity. Will we recognize each other, even in our glorified, resurrection bodies? Yes! How will you know me if I don't have a bald head? I don't know, but I'm sure you will recognize me, even with all of my curly, dark hair!

... Now I know in part, but then I shall know just as I also am known.

What will it be like to know to the same degree that we are also known? There's no way to tell ahead of time; we'll simply have to experience it. In God's presence we will all have perfect knowledge and we will need no introductions. You will know Moses and Elijah and Miriam and Deborah and David and all the rest—and they will know you—without the need for a single introduction. Glorious!

... And now abide faith, hope, love, these three;

This potent trio endures. Faith is believing whatever God says. Even in heaven, we will continue to believe what God has said. We will continue to trust in Him. So faith abides. It remains. It will always be present.

Hope is a combination of desire and expectation. Both elements have to be present for it to qualify as biblical hope. One Old Testament prophet called us "prisoners of hope" (Zechariah 9:12). We hope in the glory of the Lord. We *desire* the glory of the Lord and we also *expect* the glory of the Lord.

Hope keeps you going when everything around you is failing. "Hang in there, the Lord is going to work! Expect Him to work. Desire Him to work. It will happen." Hope keeps you and sustains you.

... but the greatest of these is love.

Why is love the greatest of the three? Because it fully encompasses the other two. Remember that "love believes all things," so faith is encompassed in love. In addition, "love hopes all things," so love encompasses hope as well. Thus, the greatest is love. The greatest thing you can possess is *agape* love. Quite simply, it has and always will reign supremely.

Test Yourself

The apostle Paul not only promoted *agape* love; he also promoted self-examination, particularly among those called to demonstrate such love. "But let a man examine himself... for if we would judge ourselves we would not be judged" (1 Corinthians 11:28, 31). "Examine yourselves ... test yourselves" (2 Corinthians 13:5).

And the Bible's great "Love Chapter" gives you a tremendous opportunity for self-examination.

To take this test, go back through 1 Corinthians 13, remove the word "love" or "charity" wherever they appear, and insert your own name. "Chuck suffers long and is kind. Chuck does not envy. Chuck does not parade himself, is not puffed up," and so on.

As you start going down the list, you may begin to gulp and say, "Oops! It doesn't fit. Chuck never fails?" Go ahead and laugh—but put your own name in there!

Once you've done that, go back through the passage once more. This time, put the name of Jesus in place of *agape*: "Jesus suffers long and is kind. Jesus does not envy. Jesus does not parade Himself, is not puffed up. Jesus does not behave rudely. Jesus does not seek His own. Jesus is not provoked. Jesus thinks no evil. Jesus does not rejoice in iniquity, but rejoices in the truth. Jesus bears all things, believes all things, hopes all things, endures all things. Jesus never fails."

It fits, doesn't it? It just flows.

This little exercise can serve as a great test to see how far down the road you have traveled toward what the Lord would have you to be. He wants the very *agape* love He demonstrates all the time to be vitally at work in your own life. And if you find you don't have love, then all of the spiritual giftings you might have are meaningless.

Love Endures

Years ago we went out to the Orange County Airport to pick up my dad and brother, who were to fly in on a private plane. When we waited more than an hour beyond the estimated time of arrival, we began to worry that they might have crashed.

They had picked an extremely stormy November night to fly up from San Diego. We knew they had to go around Camp Pendleton, so we wondered if they might have crashed in the ocean. From our hometown of Huntington Beach, we could hear the surf crashing and the waves pounding—and we had little trouble picturing them out there in the wild ocean.

Through the night we tossed and turned, wondering and hoping that the phone would ring, bringing us news that they had safely landed at some remote airstrip. Maybe they landed miles from a phone and had no opportunity to call? Maybe, somehow, they had survived? We clung to that hope, that little glimmer of hope, through the long, wild, stormy night.

In the morning the phone did ring. A man from the Civil Air Patrol told us the plane had been found; it had crashed at Camp Pendleton. There were no survivors.

As my glimmer of hope went out, the awesome realization that I would never again hug my dad rushed in. I would never again ski with my brother. I wouldn't be able to share ideas and love and thoughts with either of them ever again in this world.

Immediately I had a sinking feeling, a hopeless feeling, a terrible feeling. I cannot really describe it. The only hope I had left pertained to the future, when by the grace of God I knew I'd join them in Jesus' kingdom. But oh, I remember the forlorn and empty feeling as our hope was taken away, even a hope without any rational basis.

"And now abide faith, hope, love, these three;" Paul writes, "but the greatest of these is love."

Love never fails. It remains despite tragedy, despite hardship, despite disappointment, even despite death. Some hopes fade, but my love for my dad and my brother still remains as strong as ever. Love endures. And I know that God longs for us to express His never-failing *agape* love to everyone around us—and none of us knows for just how long we'll have them around. So that means the best time for us to direct God's love to them is always *now*.

Love in Action

A CERTAIN FELLOW FANCIED himself as an art critic. He loved to go to galleries and show off all of his knowledge with his friends. He would stroll through the halls, talking about the Van Goghs and their color mixtures and the way the artist used light and a thousand other details—all just to show off his vast understanding of art.

He'd approach one artist's work and say, "Do you see what's wrong with this painting?" or "He clearly didn't use the right technique here" or "Obviously, he doesn't understand perspective."

He was just one of those types of guys.

However, as he got a little older, he became somewhat nearsighted. One day he was walking through the art gallery with his friends, pontificating about each painting, most of it from memory. Finally he positioned himself in front of a new work and said, "Now, *why* an artist would choose such a stupid-looking model is beyond me!" And he started verbally tearing to pieces what he saw in the frame—until his wife sidled up next to him and said, "Honey, you're looking in a mirror."

Remember what James said?

> But be doers of the Word, and not hearers only, deceiving yourselves. For if anyone is a hearer of the Word and not a doer, he is like a man observing his natural face in a mirror; for he observes himself, goes away, and immediately forgets what kind of man he was (James 1:22-24).

When you leave the mirror, pretty soon you think you're good-looking. You forget the truth of what you saw. You forget the flaws. "Be doers of the Word," says James.

The spiritual application should be clear. Here I am, claiming to be a child of God who loves the Lord Jesus Christ, born again by the Spirit of God. But do I have the fruit of the Spirit bursting forth from my life? That's the question. Can I say that God's love resides in my heart and is pouring out to others?

God calls you and me to love as He loves. He wants the Spirit to flow forth from us. He longs for the fruit of the Spirit to blossom in our hearts. But for that to happen, we need to abide in Christ and get His Word abiding in us.

God has promised that if we walk in the Spirit, then we will not fulfill the lust of the flesh. If we walk in the Spirit, then the fruit of the Spirit will grow in our lives. If we're led by the Spirit, then God's *agape* love will burst forth.

Counterfeits Hurt

Those who falsely claim to be born-again have always hurt the church. They do great damage when they claim to be Christians but never demonstrate God's love. The world mocks such counterfeits—and rightly so. It laughs because of all the fighting, bickering, backbiting, and unholy competition it sees in the church. A person of the world looks on organized religion and says, "Hey, why do I need *that*? I have that in my own home. I don't need to go to church to find that stuff."

God calls you to manifest His love to others. He wants this to be a practical reality in your life, not just some theoretical ideal. He calls you to yield yourself to the Spirit of God so that His love might come forth. He wants you to abide in Him, to develop your relationship with Him, so that His words begin to abide in you. When you hang in there with Him, God's love will be perfected in your life.

And so shall you be His disciple.

It does no good to say, "Oh my, what a nice way to live! Wouldn't that be wonderful?" but then turn right around after church and say, "Listen, do you know what *he* did? Do you know what *she* said to me?" And instead of loving, you start biting and devouring and tearing down.

Meanwhile, the Spirit continues to say, "My child, this isn't some fanciful theory. This kind of love is what God wants in you and for you. How can you claim to be a follower of Jesus and yet not have His love flowing through you to others?"

One Fruit, Many Tastes

If 1 Corinthians 13 describes and defines God's *agape* love, then Galatians 5:22-23 illustrates what that love looks like in action. To get a better idea of how God wants us to love others, let's briefly consider each part of this crucial passage.

> *But the fruit of the Spirit is love …*

Immediately before Paul launches into his discussion of the fruit of the Spirit, he spends some time describing what he calls "the works of the flesh." It is not a pretty list: adultery, fornication, uncleanness, lewdness, idolatry, sorcery, hatred, contentions, jealousies, outbursts of wrath, selfish ambitions, dissensions, heresies, envy, murders, drunkenness, revelries, "and the like." Nor do those who engage in such vile behavior have a pretty future to anticipate: "those who practice such things will not inherit the kingdom of God" (Galatians 5:19-21).

Happily, Paul says, God has a much better way of life planned for His children. The fruit of the Spirit contrasts sharply with the works of the flesh. While the works end in death, the fruit brings life.

And notice something interesting here. Paul talks about the *works* of the flesh, plural, but the *fruit* of the Spirit, singular. While he uses nine terms to describe the fruit of the Spirit, in reality there is only one fruit of the Spirit: *agape* love. The other eight words simply picture *agape* in action.

Perhaps you have heard some say that just as there are nine gifts of the Spirit, so are there nine fruits of the Spirit. But in fact, there are *more* than nine gifts of the Spirit and only *one* fruit of the Spirit, which is love. The other eight qualities listed after love in Galatians 5:22-23—joy, peace, longsuffering, kindness, goodness, faithfulness, gentleness and self-control—are simply characteristics of *agape*, the kind of love God calls His children to show to the world.

As we begin our brief exploration of the fruit of the Spirit, let us recall once more that the kind of love God calls us to manifest is not the Greek *eros*, nor the Greek *phileo*, but *agape*. This word more or less is coined in the New Testament to describe a depth of divine love beyond the ability of any mere human to develop. This self-giving, all-consuming love originates in God and flows out through His people as they yield to His Spirit. And so the fruit of the Spirit is love,

. . . joy,

Have you watched a couple in love? Maybe you saw them walking hand-in-hand on a dreary, smoggy day. "Good morning," you said to them.

"Oh," they replied in unison, "isn't it just a glorious, beautiful day?" So much joy! Why? Because of love. Joy is love's consciousness.

When you're in love with the Lord, nothing seems like drudgery. No task you do for Him seems like work. It's such a joy to know Him and to be walking with Him. Your love for Him brings you a clear consciousness of His greatness and majesty and undying love for you—and that brings you great joy.

... peace,

This *agape* love is full of peace, which means far more than the absence of war.

Suppose you get involved with two guys who have been trying to beat each other's brains out. You move in, separate them, and get them on opposite sides of the room. Finally you say, "Thank goodness, we've restored peace."

But have you really? They're still glaring at each other, still snarling and gnashing their teeth at one another, just waiting for the restraints to be lifted so they can move in for the kill. That isn't true peace. Genuine peace does not come until love arrives. Only when you begin to love can you have true peace in your heart and genuine peace in your life.

... longsuffering,

What does it mean to be longsuffering? We looked briefly at this word in another chapter, but an alternate way to translate the term is to use the word "long-tempered." While not many people know what long-tempered is, probably all of us know something about its opposite. If I tell you I'm "short-tempered," you immediately know what I mean. You know that you had better not cause me to stub my toe, even accidentally, because if you do, I'll let you have it.

Someone who is truly longsuffering might think, *Man, I've taken it, I've taken it, and I've taken it, and now I'd really like to do something about it—but I know that's just my flesh talking. This person doesn't need my wrath; she needs my love. So if I have to put up with a little more of this, then so be it. May God help me!*

Agape love takes, and takes, and takes, and still remains mellow. It doesn't look for revenge. It doesn't say, "I'm through taking my share; now I'm going to dish some out." That isn't true love. Genuine *agape* is longsuffering.

... *kindness,*

A kind person is sensitive to another's needs. So many times we are so into ourselves that we don't even listen to the problems of others. Have you ever tried to tell somebody about something unpleasant that happened to you, and you quickly see they're not even listening? As soon as you're through speaking, they immediately start talking about something completely different, as if they hadn't heard a word you just said.

"How are you today?" they may ask.

"Well," you reply, "I'm not too good. My child is sick and I feel terrible."

"Oh, well, I was thinking that if I went over to John's place later today...."

They didn't even hear you! They show no sensitivity, no real interest in you at all. They're so interested in themselves that they're not even listening.

We often need someone just to talk to. We need the caring ear of someone who will show interest in us and in our problems, who will listen and remain sensitive and display some sympathy toward our unfortunate situation.

Such a need to be heard often strikes us in the middle of a big crowd. Maybe you come to church early one Sunday and sit down before the service, hoping to speak with someone. But everybody seems to walk in with their little cliques, and there you sit, alone. You feel like screaming, "Does *anybody* here want to talk to me? I need someone to listen to me!" But most of us don't come into the service looking to be kind. We come to be fed, and our insensitivity shows.

"Oh, there's Jane. Hello, friend. How are you doing?" And so we stand up and wave, putting ourselves directly in front of the hurting person—and he or she continues to sit there, just wishing *someone* would notice their hurt.

Agape love is kind. It's sensitive. It senses another person's need—and it has a genuine interest in trying to meet that need.

. . . goodness,

I do not believe that a law makes anybody good. In fact, I doubt that good people need laws. Only bad people need laws. If everyone were obedient, then you wouldn't need any laws, except maybe for things like traffic control and other community regulations designed for public safety. Laws are typically for bad people. Laws cannot make anybody good. They might restrain someone from doing evil, but they don't make anyone a better person.

"Oh, isn't Johnny a good boy?" some observer says at a Sunday service. "Just look at the way he sits there, so polite and so quiet."

Maybe. But what if his dad had said to him, "If you so much as twitch one finger, I'm going to knock your head off when we get out of here"? In that case, you don't really know if Johnny's good or not. He might be only scared.

Or imagine someone comes up to me and says, "Hey, you're a pastor. You have to be good."

I may smile, but I feel like replying, "You know what? I'll be what I want to be. I don't have to take orders from *you*." So am I really good, or not?

But what if someone comes up to me and says, "Chuck, you have two sons who are watching everything you do. When they grow up, they're going to be the same kind of man that they see in you." Because I love my sons, I want to do only that which will lead them into the right kind of life. I don't want to set a bad example for them.

And that is why love really is the strongest motive to goodness.

... faithfulness,

Agape love has a trustworthy character about it. The person who displays this element of love is faithful. You never have to worry about him turning against you. You never have to worry about her breaking her promises. You never have to worry about him going behind your back and trying to destroy you. She is trustworthy. He is faithful. And that wonderful quality grows out of a heart of love.

The Bible tells us to confess our faults to one another (James 5:16), but it doesn't ask us to check our brains at the door in the process. You need to be very careful about choosing who gets to hear your confessions! A lot of people cannot be trusted with sensitive information. I know many folks who have burdened themselves with real trouble over these kinds of tell-all confessional episodes. A lot of hurt and damage can result if you don't make certain that the person about to hear your confession is trustworthy.

I heard a story about three ministers who got together to purge their consciences by confessing their sins to each other. The first minister said, "I have a problem with drinking. Nobody knows this, but I always keep a bottle at home. I'm just a private drinker, not a social drinker. But I have to have my bottle, and every night before I go to bed, I have a drink or two."

The next minister said, "My problem is women. I just cannot seem to get free of lust! I have a strong desire to be with beautiful women. It's really terrible. I don't know what I'm going to do."

The third minister said, "Well, my sin is gossip, and I just cannot *wait* to get out of here!"

Be careful. You don't know who might have the sin of gossip. Make your confession only to someone you can trust, to an individual who has your best interests at heart. While I've been burned many times because I have trusted someone who turned out to be untrustworthy, I continue to pray, "God, never make me jaundiced toward my brothers in Christ." I'd rather trust and get burned than refuse to trust.

Not to a ridiculous extent, of course. If some guy comes up to me and says, "Hey, man, I've got a genuine Rolex watch here. I need money to get home. Can you give me a hundred bucks for it?" I'm trusting, but not stupid.

Even more, however, I want to be trustworthy. I want to be found faithful. I want to remain so in love with God that people know they can trust me to act for their good and never for their hurt.

... gentleness,

The word "gentleness" has much in common with humility and meekness. I believe that true humility is largely unconscious of itself. Every once in a while I hear someone say, "We're just doing the best we can in our humble little way"—and instantly I know that person is just about the proudest person for five miles around.

If you're really humble, then you're not proud of the fact that you're humble. I know that in Numbers 12:3 Moses apparently wrote of himself, "Now the man Moses was very humble, more than all men who were on the face of the earth," but he never let his humility go to his head. He had too close of a relationship to God for that. He knew how small he really was.

Agape love allows you to give and serve without keeping accounts. It prevents you from seeking to elevate yourself or looking to jump ahead of the pack. It doesn't keep saying, "You know, I did it for you." It gives and serves because that is its nature, not because it is looking for something really nice in return.

Gentleness is crucial when you're involved in the process of restoring a fallen believer. In fact, immediately after Paul wrote about the fruit of the Spirit, he added, "Brethren, if a man is overtaken in any trespass, you who are spiritual restore such a one in a spirit of gentleness, considering yourself lest you also be tempted" (Galatians 6:1).

God never desires to condemn the sinner, but always seeks to restore him. And if I take the attitude of condemning everybody who does wrong, then I'm not taking God's attitude toward people. How sad that so many people seem to think God wants to condemn everyone who does something wrong! That is not His nature at all. God wants to restore everyone who has fallen in some way—and He wants *us* to help in the process by displaying a gentle, meek spirit. Humility says, "Given the right circumstances, I could just as easily have fallen as you did. I cannot stand in judgment of you."

If you are going to be a servant of God, walking in love, then you must seek to help in that restoration process. Gentleness does not say, "Well, I knew that guy was a flake, anyhow." God calls us to restore sinners in a spirit of meekness, not to show up with a haughty spirit. Who are we to lay down the heavy hand of the law by saying, "*How* could you do that? What were you thinking, man?"

To restore someone in a spirit of gentleness means realizing, *Hey, I'm capable of doing the same thing. Were it not for the grace of God and the power of God's Spirit, I could be guilty of the very same thing—or worse.*

God's love is gentle. Humble. Meek. And it's what He expects of us.

... self-control,

Someone who lives with self-control values moderation in all things. They're not extravagant in dress or in jewelry or in spending or in recreational pursuits. *The King James Bible* uses the word "temperance" to translate the underlying Greek term, but to modern readers temperance suggests merely an aversion to alcohol. Yet a man can be a teetotaler and be very intemperate. An intemperate woman might never let alcohol touch her lips, and yet be mean and brash and over the top in many other ways. A self-controlled individual tends to be mellow and moderate because he or she has learned to crucify the flesh and to control his or her basic instincts.

Whenever I see a professing believer or organization working overtime to discredit or injure another believer or ministry, I have a pretty good idea that self-control has taken a hiatus. The flesh has the upper hand and havoc will shortly ensue.

I just don't know what gets into professing believers who feel called of God to tear down another believer or ministry. When someone tries to build up his or her position by tearing down others, it is merely a work of the flesh—and no believer gets to that point without a serious lack of self-control.

I'm not much into the Internet, but I understand that it presents tremendous potential for evil. I understand why they call it "the Web"—it's terribly easy to get badly entangled in that thing. And because of its anonymity, people seem to exercise very little restraints over what they view, read, or say. They can secretly post all kinds of lies and rumors on the net, and who can challenge them?

I know of some individuals and groups who call themselves Christian, and yet their whole Internet presence appears designed only to tear down and not build up the body of Christ. Their sites overflow with what the Bible would call biting and devouring. But as the Word says, biting and devouring does nothing but destroy parts of the body of

Christ. I believe the Web—when self-control is missing—can be a powerful tool of the enemy to set the church in opposition against each other. And that is tragic.

I know there are many good, apologetic ministries who have web sites on the Internet. And some of the faith's best minds are involved in apologetics. But unfortunately, many of these fellows have a way of turning on each other and using their brilliant minds for undermining other apologists or ministries. And I'm quite sure that when this happens, Satan just sits back, chuckling, as he gets them to oppose, tear down, bite and devour one another.

We must be very careful of all of that. A little self-control will go a long way toward defusing one of the enemy's most lethal weapons.

No Law Against Love

Paul wrapped up his potent dissertation on the fruit of the Spirit by writing, "Against such there is no law." There is no law telling you that you can only be so kind, but no kinder. No legal injunction prevents you from becoming too good. No judge will say, "Sorry, but you must be less faithful than that."

There is no law against love.

If you have love, you will not be doing the wicked things that laws are created to discourage. Love is the fulfilling of the law. If you choose to put your love into action by displaying the fruit of the Spirit in all its lovely forms, then you will be manifesting God to everyone around you. It's really that simple.

In the sixth chapter of Galatians, Paul extends this line of thought when he writes, "Bear one another's burdens, and so fulfill the law of Christ" (6:2). And how do we bear one another's burdens? We take practical steps to act in someone else's best interests. That is, we love them by manifesting the fruit of the Spirit on their behalf. And in that way, we fulfill the law of Christ.

Jesus lived this way, even to the very end. He bore your burdens for you, all the way to the cross. So Peter can confidently encourage you to cast "all your care upon Him, for He cares for you" (1 Peter 5:7). Just as Jesus was willing to bear your burden, so now you need to bear the burdens of others. That's how you fulfill the law of Christ.

Remember, when one member of Christ's body suffers, we all suffer (1 Corinthians 12:26). Within His body, therefore, we need to develop a keen sensitivity for ministering more effectively to each other. When a brother is hurting, we need to learn how to stand with him and encourage him and support him. When a sister has a heavy load she must carry, we have to train ourselves how to best step in and help her to bear her burden. That's what the Lord would have us to do. That's what *agape* love has a burning desire to do.

The Rewards of Agape in Ministry

I have to tell you, the rewards of the gospel ministry are fantastic. Every week I receive glorious letters from people whose lives have been blessed by the teaching of the Word of God. What a blessing I get when people describe what God is doing in their lives through the ministry of the Word. I hear these things and I am blessed.

In fact, God has blessed me in every way possible. He has blessed me physically with good health. He has blessed me spiritually in my walk with Him. He has blessed me emotionally. He has blessed me in every possible way. God takes very good care of me!

And so I love to go out and minister God's love and truth to people without charge. I suppose I've followed Paul in this way (1 Corinthians 9:18). It's fun for me when people ask, "How much do you charge to come?" and I can say, "I've never charged anybody." Whenever people ask about my expenses, I always tell them, "Look, my Father is extremely wealthy. He takes care of all of my needs. So you don't have to worry about taking care of me; my Father has given me a lavish expense account." God is good! He has abundantly blessed me, for which I give Him thanks.

But beyond all question, the greatest blessing of all is to be able to redistribute to others some of the *agape* love He has shown me. There's just no question about it. That is the greatest thrill of my life. It's the very best thing of all.

So let's walk in love, be led by the Spirit and live in the Spirit. That's the secret to a life of love, joy, peace, longsuffering, kindness, goodness, faithfulness, gentleness, and self-control. In other words, that's the secret to the good life.

Love Tested

ONE OF THE HARDEST things in the world for me to do is to walk around the church grounds picking up cigarette butts. I grew up with a mother who constantly told me how dirty cigarettes were and how I should never touch them. Her conviction so thoroughly embedded itself in my brain—never even to lay a finger on the filthy things—that I still find it extremely hard to reach down and pick up cigarette butts.

Fortunately, the church got me a little grabber tool so I no longer have to touch them. And while that makes it a lot easier on me, I still found myself thinking, *People who smoke are so dirty! They throw cigarette butts on the ground and then twist them into the sidewalk with their foot. Disgusting!* As I walked around the grounds cleaning up after them, I would gripe, complain, and generally have a bad attitude.

One day as I was getting ready to pick up yet another cigarette butt, the Lord spoke to me. I had been going through my regular routine, getting upset at people who would do such things.

"Who are you doing that for?" the Lord asked me.

"Well, Lord," I replied, "it's for You. It's Your church and I don't want it to look trashy."

"If you're really doing it for Me," He said, "then quit your complaining."

I had been telling myself for such a long time that I picked up those cigarette butts for Him, that I actually considered it the truth. God had to point out to me that whatever I do for Him, I should do it with joy. My griping only proved that I *wasn't* really doing it for Him; I was doing it for myself. But I had repeated the lie for so long that I had come to believe it.

Believing the Lie

Have you ever known someone who has told a lie so often he's come to believe it himself? It really does happen. In fact, it happens quite often in the spiritual realm.

A lot of people make professions of faith in Jesus Christ. It's easy to say very deeply-devoted kinds of things about the Lord. It's easy to talk about my dedication to God with swelling words of great commitment. But too often, there's nothing behind the words.

And so the apostle John gave us a series of tests designed to help us measure what we say against reality. This is very important, because the Bible tells us that our hearts are deceitful above all things and desperately wicked (Jeremiah 17:9). Scripture warns us repeatedly against self-deception. John is particularly good here, because he highlights the key issues that people oftentimes boast about, and then gives several tests to help us judge whether our profession matches the truth.

Throughout his first epistle, John uses the word *agape* to describe the kind of love he has in mind. As we have seen, this love on the spiritual level is a totally giving love, especially of itself. The object of this love is people. When *agape* lives in me, I love people so much; I'm interested only in their best welfare. I want only what is good and best for them and their needs. The paramount thing on my mind is giving to them, without looking for something in return—just like God's love.

So the question for us is not simply, "Do I claim to love God? Do I claim to love others as He loves them?" The question is rather, "What evidence do I have to prove that my love for God and others is real?"

Two Kinds of "Knowing"

How can I really *know* that I know God? Many people say, "I know Him," but their claims do not necessarily hold up under investigation. The first epistle of John uses the term "know" more than thirty times, involving two Greek words.

Some twenty times, the word "know" comes from the Greek term *ginosko*, which is to know by experience. If you put your finger in a live electrical socket, you'll get a terrific jolt. I know this well because when I was a little boy, I curiously put my finger in an open socket—and still I can remember the jolt I got. That's *ginosko*, knowing by experience. We see this form of "knowing" illustrated in 1 John 2:3, "Now by this we know [*ginosko*] that we know [*ginosko*] Him...." John says we can know by experience that we have come into a relationship with God.

The second Greek term for "know," *oida*, appears some fourteen times in John's first letter. This term means to know by intuition or through an outside source. We know many things in our spiritual walk because the Bible declares them; we know them through faith or by intuition, by *oida*. For example, 1 John 3:2 says, "We know [*oida*] that when He shall appear, we shall be like Him." How do we know this? We cannot know it by experience, not quite yet; but we know it because the Scripture affirms it. We know it by *oida*, through intuition or faith, rather than by *ginosko*, through personal experience.

With that little background in mind, we're ready for John's tests. How can we know for sure that we love God and His people? Let's take a short walk through part of his letter to see what we might learn.

TEST ONE: KEEPING HIS COMMANDMENTS

Several times John focuses on keeping God's commandments as a test of our love for God. For example:

> Now by this we know that we know Him, if we keep His commandments. He who says, "I know Him," and does not keep His commandments is a liar, and the truth is not in him. But whoever keeps His word, truly the love of God is perfected in him. By this we know that we are in Him. He who says he abides in Him ought himself also to walk just as He walked (1 John 2:3-6).

So you claim to have had an experience with God and a relationship with Jesus Christ? What proof can you supply for your claim? The mere fact that you say so doesn't necessarily mean anything. John says that the proof is found in your obedience to Him.

We know very well what proof John had in mind. History remembers him as "John the beloved," largely because he caught the main message of Jesus—that the most important part of being a Christian is having and manifesting God's love. "A new commandment I give to you," Jesus told His disciples, "that you love one another; as I have loved you, that you also love one another" (John 13:34). John passes on to us this message of love for one another more than any other idea.

In fact, he gets pretty strong about it. He has a word for those who claim to know God and yet neglect to keep His commandments: "liar." A lot of people go around saying, "I know God," and yet they're filled with hatred. They speak with evil intent and seek to degrade others. John calls you a liar if you say that you know Him and yet do not keep His commandments, especially His supreme command to love one another. If you say you have received Jesus into your life, and yet harbor bitterness or hatred for your brother or sister, then you're lying.

But the opposite is also true. If you really are keeping His commandments through the power of the Holy Spirit, then the love of God is being perfected in you. The word "perfected" means completed, fully developed.

So how do you know you're in Him? You know it because God's love is being perfected in your life. Since God's love for you is better than unconditional, that means the love being perfected in you will also be better than unconditional.

And what did John mean by "walking as Jesus walked"? Peter gives us a clue when he writes, "For to this you were called, because Christ also suffered for us, leaving us an example, that you should follow His steps: 'Who committed no sin, nor was deceit found in His mouth;' who, when He was reviled, did not revile in return; when He suffered, He did not threaten, but committed Himself to Him who judges righteously" (1 Peter 2:21-23). That's the example that Jesus set for you to follow; that's how you are to walk. "This is My commandment," Jesus said, "that you love one another as I have loved you" (John 15:12). Jesus taught us that love is supreme, so love is the real proof of your relationship with Jesus. Love is the ultimate proof that you truly are a child of God.

Toward the end of his letter, John once again revisited this key idea:

> By this we know that we love the children of God, when we love God and keep His commandments (1 John 5:2).

This time around, John reverses the spin on his comments. His question now is not, "How can I know that I love God?" but rather, "How can I know that I love the children of God?" He knows that it's all too easy for us to say, "I love humanity! It's people I cannot stand." So he takes us back to the basics.

He reminds us that love for God and love for people go hand-in-hand. You don't answer the question, "Do I really love people?" by asking yourself how you feel about them. You answer the question by asking how eagerly and thoroughly you've been obeying God's commandments—especially ones like, "Love your enemies; bless those who curse you; do good to those who hate you; and pray for those who spitefully use you and persecute you."

And why should I do that, Jesus? He answers, "That you may be sons of your Father in heaven" (Matthew 5:44-45).

TEST TWO: LOVING ONE ANOTHER

John's most frequent exhortations in this letter call for followers of Christ to love their brothers and sisters in the Lord. Let's take a look at several of these texts.

> He who says he is in the light, and hates his brother, is in darkness until now. He who loves his brother abides in the light, and there is no cause for stumbling in him. But he who hates his brother is in darkness and walks in darkness, and does not know where he is going, because the darkness has blinded his eyes (1 John 2:9-11).

The proof that you "abide in the light" once more comes back to the issue of love, specifically the love of your brother. Sometimes when I overhear someone say some very derogatory things about another person, I'll say, "You really hate them; don't you?" And how do you suppose they usually respond? "Oh no, no, I don't hate them! I love them." *Really*? Because if you really love someone, you're not apt to say such mean, cruel, cutting things; are you? Paul tells us, "Speak evil of no man" (Titus 3:2). So how do we know that we've passed from the darkness of Satan into the brilliant light of God? We know it when we love our brothers.

And then John takes it a step further:

> We know that we have passed from death to life, because we love the brethren. He who does not love his brother abides in death. Whoever hates his brother is a murderer, and you know that no murderer has eternal life abiding in him (1 John 3:14-15).

You can be very busy with church activities and still feel very resentful toward others who haven't come along to help you. Remember my cigarette butts? As you are doing these things "for the Lord," you can be grumbling, complaining, and griping that no one else is stepping up to assist you, and in your mind you can go through fits of anger against your brothers and sisters. You don't love them; John says quite bluntly that you "hate" them.

And then he dares to call you a murderer, devoid of eternal life.

Jesus came into conflict with the Pharisees over this very issue of demonstrating genuine, divine love. Although these religious leaders kept the law outwardly, they were vicious inwardly. And thus they had contempt for anyone who failed to live by the standards and rules they themselves had set up. Inevitably they butted heads with Jesus, because He constantly stressed the inner attitudes of the heart.

God is far more interested in your heart than in your outward actions. The Pharisees taught, "You shall not murder," but Jesus taught, "I say to you that whoever is angry with his brother without a cause shall be in danger of the judgment. And whoever says to his brother, 'Raca!' [vain fellow] shall be in danger of the council. But whoever says, 'You fool!' shall be in danger of hell fire" (Matthew 5:22). When you look with disdain on another person, you're just as guilty of murder as the one who has killed an innocent victim. Although we tend to look on the outward appearance, God looks at the heart.

When you love the brethren, you prove that you really are a child of God. God has put that love for the family of God in your heart: "We know that we have passed from death to life, because we love the brethren."

And remember that the kind of love John has in mind here is *agape*, God's self-giving love that manifests itself in practical, supportive actions. So John writes:

> But whoever has this world's goods, and sees his brother in need, and shuts up his heart from him, how does the love of God dwell in him? My little children, let us not love in word or in tongue, but in deed and in truth. And by this we know that we are of the truth, and shall assure our hearts before Him (1 John 3:17-19).

While you probably will never be asked to lay down your life for your Christian brother, how about giving a part of your livelihood for someone in need? That's how real love is demonstrated, in practical ways. It's not merely a theoretical thing; this is where the rubber meets the road.

Words are fine, but they're not nearly enough. When someone has a real need that you can help meet, how does it help to pat the person on the back and say, "Well, God bless you, brother. I trust everything will work out for you"? John would say, "How does the love of God dwell in you?"

Jesus manifested His love in loving deeds. He didn't come to earth and say, "Oh, I love you *so* much! Now go to hell." But He showed His love by dying on the cross and taking our sins upon Himself so that we *wouldn't* have to go to hell.

What do I profit a brother in need if I don't give him a coat or a blanket or some food or shelter? When we love in deeds, we love in truth. Loving in words alone won't cut it. I always get a little suspicious when someone says to me, "Oh, I love you so much, brother," every time I see him. One fellow around Calvary Chapel said that to me for a long time—and then he did his best to put a knife in my back. Let's love in action and by what we do, in reaching out, in helping, in giving a call, in giving a word of encouragement, in giving financial support. Let's reach out in love to touch each other and to help each other. Let's love in deed, for that's love in truth.

Best of all, when we love in this way, our actions give us confidence and assurance that we do indeed have a genuine experience with God. That's how we know—*ginosko*, to know by experience—that we know the Lord. "And by this we know that we are of the truth, and shall assure our hearts before Him."

John wants to make so sure that we *get* this point, he emphasizes it again and again. So once more in chapter 4 he encourages us:

> Beloved, let us love one another, for love is of God; and everyone who loves is born of God and knows God. He who does not love does not know God, for God is love (1 John 4:7-8).

I have heard people say, "Hey, I know that I have the Spirit of God, because I speak in tongues!" You don't know any such thing.

Speaking in tongues is no proof that the Spirit of God abides in you. Satan can counterfeit tongues. The only real proof that the Spirit of God abides in you is love.

You know the Spirit of God dwells within you when you see His fruit in your life, especially a great love for your brothers and sisters in Christ. I tell the folks at Calvary Chapel, "If you can love me, then you know that you've got the Spirit!" If you see the Spirit's fruit of love in your life, then you know with certainty that the Spirit of God lives within you. Love is something that Satan just cannot counterfeit.

Okay, then, but what is to be the standard of our love? John insists that it's to be the very love of God itself:

> Beloved, if God so loved us, we also ought to love one another. No one has seen God at any time. If we love one another, God abides in us, and His love has been perfected in us (1 John 4:11-12).

The Scriptures often exhort us to look to Christ as our example in both forgiveness and in love. We are to love as He loved and forgive as He forgave. Paul wrote,

> And be kind to one another, tenderhearted, forgiving one another, even as God in Christ forgave you (Ephesians 4:32).

Now, that's a pretty big order! And yet that is exactly what God requires of us—and just what God's Spirit will enable us to do as He perfects His love in us.

As we dwell in love, God dwells in us. And because His essence is love, that love gets perfected in us over time. How wonderful to see God's love becoming perfected in our lives. At one time I thought I could never get along with a certain fellow. And yet, as God's Spirit worked within me, giving me His love, God joined me together with that man to make him one of the most dear friends I have ever known. How thrilling to experience God's love perfected in us.

And yet John doesn't want us to go too far off into the "loving" stratosphere. It's great to speak of feeling thrilled over God perfecting His love in us, but John much prefers our love to remain grounded by connection to real life and real people. So he writes:

> If someone says, "I love God," and hates his brother, he is a liar; for he who does not love his brother whom he has seen, how can he love God whom he has not seen? And this commandment we have from Him: that he who loves God must love his brother also (1 John 4:20-21).

Earlier John had written that anyone who claimed to know God but didn't keep His commandments was a liar. Now he writes that anyone who says he loves God but hates his brother is a liar. Pretty blunt! If you say you love God, then you must love your brother also; and if you don't love your brother, then you're a liar.

You cannot love God and hate your brother. If you confess that you love God and yet you do hate your brother, you're being deceived.

You're living a lie. The truth isn't in you. Here's the commandment: love God. If you love God, then love your brother.

We need to remember what Jesus said would happen when He returns to earth in power and glory. He said He would separate the sheep from the goats, placing the sheep—those who honored and obeyed Him—on His right side, and those who didn't—the goats—on His left.

> Then the King will say to those on His right hand, "Come, you blessed of My Father, inherit the kingdom prepared for you from the foundation of the world: for I was hungry and you gave Me food; I was thirsty and you gave Me drink; I was a stranger and you took Me in; I was naked and you clothed Me; I was sick and you visited Me; I was in prison and you came to Me."
>
> Then the righteous will answer Him, saying, "Lord, when did we see You hungry and feed You, or thirsty and give You drink? When did we see You a stranger and take You in, or naked and clothe You? Or when did we see You sick, or in prison, and come to You?"
>
> And the King will answer and say to them, "Assuredly, I say to you, inasmuch as you did it to one of the least of these My brethren, you did it to Me."
>
> Then He will also say to those on the left hand, "Depart from Me, you cursed, into the everlasting fire prepared for the devil and his angels: for I was hungry and you gave Me no food; I was thirsty and you gave Me no drink; I was a stranger and you did not take Me in, naked and you did not clothe Me, sick and in prison and you did not visit Me."
>
> Then they also will answer Him, saying, "Lord, when did we see You hungry or thirsty or a stranger or naked or sick or in prison, and did not minister to You?"
>
> Then He will answer them, saying, "Assuredly, I say to you, inasmuch as you did not do it to one of the least of these, you did not do it to Me."
>
> And these will go away into everlasting punishment, but the righteous into eternal life (Matthew 25:34-46).

Examine your own heart right now. Does anyone come to mind whom you have to confess you hate? If so, then God's love is not yet perfected in your life. I encourage you to bring that hatred to the Lord. Ask Him to take it away. Ask Him to perfect His love in you, especially His love for this person. Ask Him to fill you with the Spirit of God and make His love complete in your life.

It's the only way you can "know" for sure that you belong to Him.

TEST THREE: ABIDING IN THE SPIRIT

None of us can love with God's *agape* love unless His Spirit dwells within our hearts. We just don't have it within ourselves. *Agape* has to come to us from outside ourselves, from the eternal fountain of God's own overflowing love. So John writes,

> And by this we know that He abides in us, by the Spirit whom He has given us (1 John 3:24).

> By this we know that we abide in Him, and He in us, because He has given us of His Spirit (1 John 4:13).

How do you know that you're a child of God? He has imprinted His stamp of ownership, which is the Holy Spirit, upon you. Through the gift of His Spirit, God announces, "This one's Mine."

The apostle Paul in Ephesians 1:13 describes how we have been "sealed with the Holy Spirit of promise." And in 2 Corinthians 1:22 he declares that God "has sealed us and given us the Spirit in our hearts as a guarantee." So in what way is the Holy Spirit a seal and a guarantee that we belong to the Lord?

In the ancient world, Ephesus served as the major port from which goods from the east made their way west. Goods came to Ephesus overland and then were shipped by sea to Puteoli, a chief Roman port. From there they spread out to the rest of the western world.

Now, when a merchant in Ephesus bought some goods to send west, he would have them crated up and then sealed with a little hot wax, on which he would place the imprint of his signature ring. This was the sign of his ownership. When the ship finally reached Puteoli, the longshoremen knew which crates belonged to whom, because each crate bore a unique stamp of ownership.

Paul used this image of a seal to say to the Ephesians, "The Lord has put His stamp of ownership on you. He is the down payment God has given you to demonstrate His intention of redeeming you completely and fully. He has purchased you with the blood of Jesus Christ, and one day He's going to come to earth to claim ownership of His purchase. And when He does, "we shall be like Him because we shall see Him as He is" (1 John 3:2).

Oh, what a glorious future we all have in Christ Jesus! Ours is a destiny of love—perfected, made complete, and poured out through the ministry of the Holy Spirit.

The Biggest Test of All

Did you notice as we walked through these select portions of John's short letter that most of the proof of your profession of faith in Jesus Christ lies in your love for others? John repeatedly gives three general tests to determine the reality of your faith and mine:

1. Do you truly love one another?
2. Does the Holy Spirit abide in you?
3. Are you keeping God's commandments?

While the first test clearly relates to whether we love others, the second also focuses on it. For how do we know whether the Holy Spirit abides in us? Well, if God dwells in us, then love must also dwell in us, since God is love. And if it doesn't, then neither does God.

And what about keeping His commandments? We've already seen that the single divine command that encompasses all others is to love God and the people He made. So if you want proof that you're really a child of God, then the best approach is to look for evidence that you love God by noting how you love His people. Such evidence provides all the proof you need that you live in the truth, that you are walking according to truth, that you're abiding in Him, and that you are a child of God.

So—how did you do? Did you get an "A" grade? Did you score closer to a "C" average? Or maybe you gave yourself a "D" or even an "F." Whatever your current grade, God wants to work through you to bring His love to the world. He wants *you* to be a conduit of His love!

And He may well want to start by directing you to love the person you most detest.

Are you willing to let God wipe away the bitterness, the anger, the hatred that you feel toward this individual? Are you willing for the Lord to plant His love in your heart for this man or woman? I'm not asking *you* to love this person; you cannot do that any better than I can. I *am* asking if you will allow God to put His love in your heart for this individual. Are you willing to let God work in your heart to give you His love and compassion for this person?

That, my friends, is the biggest test of all.

Love as a Lifestyle

IT'S INTERESTING HOW PERSECUTION seems to bind the church together in love. While the Three-Self Movement Church of China is a puppet of the communist government, the real church there is the underground house church.

Not long ago I visited China, along with several other pastors affiliated with Calvary Chapel. We spoke in several Three-Self churches, always accompanied by a full-on communist assigned to us by the government. His job was to make sure we saw only certain things. We gave the guy a bad time, but we all had a lot of fun doing it. We realized he was just a government plant, sent to make sure unauthorized people didn't contact us.

Now, I'm a mixer. As soon as I finish speaking somewhere, I usually wade out into the crowd and start mingling. In Beijing, the people just mobbed us. The authorities got so concerned that they quickly hustled me off to a back room, where a bevy of party officials sat, looking very sober. They could all speak English, but weren't inclined to talk; they simply wanted to keep us from the people. I don't know what they were so worried about, since I don't speak a word of Chinese and the people didn't speak English. Yet we did have a beautiful connection—albeit brief—through smiles and handshakes and the universal, non-verbal language of love.

At the next Three-Self church we visited, we insisted on having our own interpreter. He had told me about all the things I never said that the government's interpreter had put in my mouth. The authorities allowed the change, but the whole time I spoke, something in the sound system made it howl with a loud, distracting wail. Still, the Spirit got through the wail and touched the people in a magnificent way. Right after the meeting ended, the people mobbed us once again. And once more the authorities quickly shooed them away and hustled us into another back room. We heard later that some people waited another two hours hoping to see us.

My son, Jeff, somehow slipped by our guards and started mixing with the crowd. He had a great time with them, while we sat in the quiet room. I count it all a very interesting experience.

The Chinese underground house church, on the other hand, has quite a different experience. Since it suffers tremendous persecution, it usually meets in secret. I recently received a letter from one of our outreaches based in Japan. Its members take Bibles and other resources into China, especially to the house church.

The woman who wrote me described how she had gone to one area where she had received an invitation to speak. When she arrived around midnight, a mystery woman met her and said to her very quietly, "Just hold on to my hand and follow me." They entered a dark room where the mystery lady said, "I will tell you when you can speak." Both women sat down in this totally dark room. Soon the guide said, "You can speak now." So the speaker taught for half an hour or so out of the Word of God.

When the meeting ended, no one said anything. The people just filed out silently into the darkness. This woman told me that by her spot next to the door, she could see just enough to count the feet of the people leaving. She counted four hundred, which meant two hundred people had been sitting in darkness, listening quietly to the Word. If the government had discovered their meeting, she said, police would have broken up the gathering, beaten the attendees, and confiscated their goods and teaching materials.

Such tough conditions tend to bring believers closer together. No one chooses to serve the Lord under such scary circumstances unless they have a genuine commitment to Him. They don't say, "Well, if it isn't raining and if I cannot find a basketball game on TV, maybe I'll go to church." Only those with a real commitment to Jesus Christ come to church in those threatening situations—and they usually develop a tremendous depth of relationship with the Lord and with each other. They share a potent bond because they realize they're in this thing together.

Ever-Increasing Love

The apostle Paul had an experience in ancient Thessalonica much like my Chinese adventure. What a great church that must have been! Paul thanked God continually for the believers there because their faith was growing exceedingly, despite their spiritual youth and the intense persecution they suffered almost immediately after their conversion. He wrote:

> But concerning brotherly love you have no need that I should write to you, for you yourselves are taught by God to love one another; and indeed you do so toward all the brethren who are in all Macedonia. But we urge you, brethren, that you increase more and more (1 Thessalonians 4:9-10).

Remember, these were young believers. Paul couldn't spend much time there—at the most a few months, at the least a few weeks. Severe persecution arose very quickly and Paul had to leave. And yet these disciples sincerely sought God and their faith grew exceedingly. We know this because Paul says their love toward each other "abounded."

Just the kind of fellowship you would like to be in!

Yes—but would you care for the persecution? Even if you knew that it was the persecution that accounted for the church's growth and love? Paul had told them, "I am thrilled that you have such a great reputation as a loving church. But even so, I want to encourage you to work at this love more and more. Let it increase!"

The mark of the true body of Christ is a great love, one believer for another. Jesus said, "By this all will know that you are My disciples, if you have love for one another" (John 13:35). A genuine love among the body of Christ not only identifies the true disciples of Jesus to the world, it also becomes a personal sign to us individually that we have passed from death to life.

Do you love the people of God? And if so, are you taking practical steps to make sure that your love increases more and more?

Love Covers a Multitude of Sins

One reason we need more and more love is that we have a lot of ugliness to deal with—and fortunately, love covers a multitude of sins.

Proverbs 10:12 says, "Hatred stirs up strife, but love covers all sins." The apostle Peter apparently had this Scripture in mind when he wrote to his fellow believers, "And above all things have fervent love for one another, for 'love will cover a multitude of sins'" (1 Peter 4:8). How does love do this covering? As a grandfather, I think I understand.

I love my grandkids. In my eyes, they can do no wrong. So what if they pour out a box of sugar on the floor? Who cares? I'll say, "Isn't that fun? Look! They've made a cute little pile out of it. They show amazing artistic ability, the way they drew in it on the floor." Love really does cover a multitude of sins.

Understand that if you're filled with hatred, everybody's going to hate you. But if you're a loving person, they're far more willing to overlook your faults. People will scrutinize the faults of a hateful person; in fact, they cannot wait to find—and point out—as many as possible. It satisfies their flesh to identify something wrong. But if you're a loving person, people tend to overlook all kinds of mistakes.

You know what this means; don't you? If you're not a perfect person, then you had better be a loving person! And one good way to practice this love is to shut your mouth.

As Proverbs 17:9 reminds us, "He who repeats a matter separates friends." When you hear some unsavory report, it's usually better to just let it go. Don't say anything about it. Overlook it in love. Rather than running around and saying, "Do you know what he did? I couldn't believe it! I stood there, just absolutely shocked!" and ruining a good friendship, just bury it. You can divide people by talking, or you can keep friends together through your loving silence. Let it go and let love cover a multitude of sins.

A Labor of Love

At the beginning of his first letter to the Thessalonians, Paul spoke of his believing friends' "labor of love" (1Thessalonians 1:3). The word for "labor" means to work to the point of weariness or exhaustion. Only God can bring that kind of labor!

How many times have you witnessed a mother scurrying around the house, laboring to the point of exhaustion, especially when her children are little? And yet it's a labor of love, because she looks at those beautiful little faces and never once thinks, *Those dirty little faces! Just throw them in bed and let it go.* She cannot help but go get the warm washcloth and the soft towel and start to lovingly wash their dirty hands, clean their messy faces and kiss their chubby cheeks, even though she is as tired as can be because all day long she's done nothing but clean up. For her, it's a labor of love, planted in her heart by a loving God.

How glorious life becomes when our love for God becomes so great that we don't even consider the weariness of our own bodies! As Paul said, "the love of Christ compels us" (2 Corinthians 5:14). It inspires us to love those who don't deserve our love. It urges us to love those who spurn our love. And it drives us to somehow love those who confuse us, who make it difficult to know *how* we can best love them.

Without question, love can be real work. It may take a lot of thought, a lot of effort, a lot of patience, a lot of creativity, a lot of trial and error, and a lot of plain old elbow grease to find the kind of love that turns the key in someone's locked-up heart. There is such a thing as a *labor* of love. And it's a job for which God hands you a "Help Wanted" ad and says, "This one is for you."

Love Your Friends

Some of the people God calls you to love are your friends. Most of the time, it's fairly easy to love them, because you like them. That's why they're your friends.

The apostle Paul had some very good friends in the ancient city of Philippi. He once wrote to them, "For God is my witness, how greatly I long for you all with the affection of Jesus Christ" (Philippians 1:8). The *King James Version* more literally translates it, "How greatly I long after you all in the bowels of Jesus Christ."

In those days people believed that the greatest human emotions came not from the brain, but from the stomach. And because they looked upon the stomach as the area of deepest feeling, they often used the phrase "bowels of mercy" or "bowels of compassion" to refer to what we might call "gut-level" emotions. Paul used that very phrase to tell the Philippians, "This is how I feel about you." He felt no shame in admitting it and clearly thought his friends would feel encouraged to hear it.

A little later in his letter he wrote, "Therefore, my beloved and longed-for brethren, my joy and crown" (Philippians 4:1). What beautiful words by Paul to his dear friends, baring his soul to them. This is the heartbeat of the apostle. He is exposing his heart, expressing in emotional language his deep love for the people to whom he ministered and who ministered to him in return. I love this!

Yet Paul's intimacy with this church seems very far removed from what we too often see today, where pastors get set high on a pedestal, aloof in an ivory tower, more or less untouchable. As Paul thinks of his friends in Philippi, however, he cries out, "I long for you, my dear friends. You're my joy and my crown."

Paul does not think of his friends simply in a fond way, nor does he intend to flatter them. Instead, he immediately puts his love to work. He tells them, "And this I pray, that your love may abound still more and more in knowledge and all discernment" (Philippians 1:9).

Love *prays*. Have you recognized that truth? Love immediately desires to connect its beloved to the God who has all power to change the loved one's circumstances for the better. "Oh Lord, help them," Paul prayed for his friends, "that the love they have for one another might increase, abounding more and more in knowledge and in all judgment."

No doubt you've heard the phrase, "To know him is to love him." The reason Jesus tells you, "Learn of Me," (Matthew 11:29) is that He wants you to know how much He loves you. So spend some time learning of Him—abound more and more in your knowledge of Him—and discover just how much He loves you. Jesus knows that the better you know Him, the more you will grasp His love for you and the greater response you will have to His love. That is how you can "abound more and more" in your love for Him and for His people.

And while you're at it, why not pray that the ones you love will have the same blessed experience!

Love Difficult People

God wants you to love your friends, but He also expects you to love the difficult people in your life. And we all have them!

The apostle Paul certainly did. While he could count on the Philippians to support and encourage him, he anticipated that the Corinthians would give him plenty of opposition and discouragement. They were his problem church.

As Jeremiah earned the title "the weeping prophet," so Paul probably could be called "the weeping apostle." He speaks often of the tears he shed over the church in Corinth and of the anguish in his heart over their poor choices. And he declared plainly in his second letter to them, "Out of much affliction and anguish of heart I wrote to you, with many tears." Why did he mention his turmoil? "Not to grieve [them] but that you might know the love which I have so abundantly for you" (2 Corinthians 2:4).

Paul is one of those individuals with whom I hope to spend a few hundred years in heaven. I've always been a great admirer of the apostle and of his ministry, so when he writes to the Corinthians, "Imitate me, just as I also imitate Christ," I accept his counsel unreservedly (1 Corinthians 11:1). I've sought to follow the example of Paul: the love he had for the church, and the concern he displayed for even the difficult people of God, his great desire to see them walking in truth and in fellowship with the Lord. I would like my own heart to mimic the great heart of the apostle Paul.

Of course, I don't pretend to come close to Paul. In writing of his tremendous love for his fellow Jews, he wrote, "For I could wish that I myself were accursed from Christ for my brethren, my countrymen according to the flesh" (Romans 9:3). That's beyond me. I cannot begin to grasp that level of concern and love. But oh, what a mighty man of God, and what a heart for God and the people of God—even the difficult people of God!

Paul wanted to make sure in his second letter that the Corinthians understood the tone of his heart as he wrote his first letter. He explained that he wrote not out of anger, but with a heart that ached for them, a heart filled with anguish, a heart filled with love—yet a heart powerfully grieving over the children whom he had brought to the Lord, children who had gone so badly astray to their own hurt.

"That heavy letter that I had to write to you," he wanted them to know, "it was hard. I did it with anguish. I wrote it with many tears." Note how the apostle bares his soul when he recalls his first letter and the response it received:

> Now I rejoice, not that you were made sorry, but that your sorrow led to repentance. For you were made sorry in a godly manner, that you might suffer loss from us in nothing. For godly sorrow produces repentance leading to salvation, not to be regretted; but the sorrow of the world produces death.
>
> For observe this very thing, that you sorrowed in a godly manner: What diligence it produced in you, what clearing of yourselves, what indignation, what fear, what vehement desire, what zeal, what vindication! In all things you proved yourselves to be clear in this matter. Therefore, although I wrote to you, I did not do it for the sake of him who had done the wrong, nor for the sake of him who suffered wrong, but that our care for you in the sight of God might appear to you (2 Corinthians 7:9-12).

No, the apostle did not find it easy to write his letter, nor did he get any pleasure from the rebuke he felt forced to give. But he loved the Corinthians—his difficult church—and therefore he expended himself in love for them. And God honored his labor of love.

Love Your Enemies

Agape asks you to love both your friends and the difficult people in your life. That can be tough enough. But then it goes a step further and instructs you to love even your enemies:

> But I say to you who hear: Love your enemies, do good to those who hate you, bless those who curse you, and pray for those who spitefully use you (Luke 6:27-28).

When you hear something like that, I imagine you're ready to argue: "Now, wait a minute, Lord! How can I love my enemies? There's no *way* I can do that. I certainly don't want to do good to those who hate me. And why should I bless those who curse me? That hardly seems fair."

Yes, these are unnatural commands. I find myself fighting against them, too. But so long as I argue with them, I will always have a shriveled spirit. I will never grow or change for the better. I'll always be trying to get even, going after the eye for an eye and the tooth for a tooth. And very soon I'll get eaten up by ulcers.

But if I will just obey—"God, I am willing, but You're going to have to love this person through me. I just cannot do it"—then I find that He will do everything for me that's required. My part is a simple willingness to obey—not to argue with Him, not to explain the injustice of it all, but just be willing to obey. And in that willingness, I discover the secret of victory. The Lord will give me the capacity and the power to obey His "impossible" commands.

No, it is *not* natural to love in this way; it's supernatural. And if you try to do it in the natural, you're going to find yourself frustrated and miserable. You cannot do it apart from the work of the Holy Spirit within your heart. Your part is to be open to the Spirit's work within you.

Love with a Sweet Spirit

Can you love someone with your fists in a tight ball, your lip curled and a snarl in your voice? Maybe you can, although I've never seen it done. That's probably why Paul wrote to young Timothy to be an example to the believers "in spirit" (1 Timothy 4:12).

God calls you to display a gentle, sweet spirit, rather than a mean, critical spirit. I know some people are just mean-spirited. It's true of dogs, too. Some dogs have a very sweet spirit. They come up to you, tail wagging and begging to be petted. They're just sweet, loving dogs. But you'll also meet dogs that will snarl and snap at you if you get too close. They're mean-spirited.

Some people, like dogs, will snap at you if you get too close. And it's interesting how some people can really be mean-spirited; I know because I frequently get letters from them. As I read their notes, I realize the writers must be absolutely miserable. They have so much anger, so much bitterness, and so much hatred pent up inside that they feel compelled to give full vent to it. Usually I just say, "God help them," as I drop their letters into the shredder.

The remarkable thing about these letters is how judgmental, critical, and condemning they usually are. I remember that Paul said, "Who is he that condemns?" clearly implying his answer: the devil. So I often think, *Well, I got another letter from the devil today. Let's just shred that and move on.*

If you have a critical spirit, I doubt you'll be happy anywhere you end up. It's like the old farmer rocking on his porch. A car came driving up with a mattress on the roof and a trailer stacked high with furniture behind. The people in the car rolled down the window and called to the farmer, "What kind of people live around here?"

"What kind of people live where you come from?" he asked, continuing to rock.

"Oh, they were mean, cantankerous, ornery folk," they replied.

"Well," he answered, "that's just the kind of people who live around here." They quickly drove off, leaving him to rock.

A few moments later another car drove up, again with a mattress on the roof and furniture stacked high in the trailer. "What kind of people live around here?" the people in the car wondered aloud.

"What kind of people live where you come from?" the farmer asked.

"Oh, they were the sweetest, most generous, most wonderful people you could ever hope to be around," they answered happily.

"Well," the old fellow said, "that's just the kind of people who live around here."

The problem, you see, is that you have to take yourself with you wherever you go. If you're mean-spirited, then you'll find your meanness following you everywhere. But if you're kind and sweet, then that's what you'll find trailing you wherever you go. It's not in other people; it's in you.

Now, be honest: If you are choosing someone to invite for coffee, and you have a choice between a mean-spirited person and a sweet-spirited person, whom are you going to choose? Not a hard choice; is it?

Remember, once you get into a critical mode, you'll have a strong tendency to criticize *everything*. Some people listen carefully to my recorded sermons—not to learn, but to find some mistake to criticize. They're constantly searching for something to find fault with, some point to condemn. It's tragic when a person gets in that critical spirit, because once you become skilled at criticizing, you're seldom good for anything else.

I believe that's why God instructs each of us to be an example to the believers in love and in spirit. A meek, quiet, gentle spirit can become a mighty tool in the hands of a loving God.

Christian, This Is Your Call

I have been privileged to minister to people of all ages, through many generations, learning to love them. The Lord has given me many experiences to learn about love through interacting with His people and by studying His Word and the character of Jesus.

Yet as much as I have attempted to love people, I know I can love them only because I have first loved God—and I can love God only because He first loved me. The reality is that in and of ourselves, we have no ability to love like Jesus. Only by God working in our lives through the Holy Spirit can we begin the quest to love as Jesus would have us love.

God-centered love is a Spirit-led love. The lack of love we see in the world and in church is not the result of people failing to love in general, but the failure of us, as the church, to love God and others through the power of the Holy Spirit. In a sense, we have not love because we ask not of the Holy Spirit for love.

The Holy Spirit is our guide in loving others. God's love is a supernatural thing that believers bring forth only by abiding and living in the Spirit. The secret to showing forth God's love lies in aligning ourselves with the Holy Spirit's desires, so that we may reflect and live out the heart and will of God toward people and toward the Lord Himself. Once we begin walking with the Spirit of God as a regular lifestyle, we can love as God would have us love.

The greatest demonstration the church can give to the world is God's love within the body, each member for the other. When we love one another with this kind of genuine, unfeigned affection, the world will take note. I know critics often say, "Oh, I don't go to church because there are too many hypocrites in the church." But to them I want to say, "Then you should not go to the movies, since there's far more hypocrisy in that crowd than there is in any church."

Nevertheless, God calls us to unfeigned love. No faking it! He instructs us through Peter, "Love one another fervently with a pure heart" (1 Peter 1:22).

"Love, love, love, love. Christian, this is your call." I still remember the old, informal days in the tent when we sang that song. We'd put our arms around each other and sing that song with all our hearts:

> Love, love, love, love. Christian, this is your call.
> Love your neighbor as yourself, for God loves all.
> Glory to God in the highest, glory to God in the highest.
> Peace on earth, goodwill toward men. Glory to God in the highest.
> King of kings and Lord of lords, King of kings forevermore.
> King of kings and Lord of lords, King of kings forever.
> Love, love, love, love. Christian, this is your call.
> Love your neighbor as yourself, for God loves all.[5]

5 *Love,* a traditional folk melody, author unknown.

EPILOGUE

And Yet There Is More

GOD LOVES YOU WITH a deep, everlasting love. That is the heart of the Bible's message. The Bible is God's revelation of Himself to humankind, and the aspect of His nature that He wishes to display above all others is love.

God loves you. And Jesus tells us how much the Father loves you: "God so loved the world that He gave His only begotten Son, that whoever believes in Him should not perish but have everlasting life" (John 3:16).

How many times in your life have you experienced the wonders of God's love? Jeremiah wrote that God demonstrates His love to you in a new way every morning. Lamentations 3:22 says,

> It is of the LORD'S mercies that we are not consumed, because His compassions fail not. They are new every morning, great is Thy faithfulness.

Peter spoke of the "manifold grace of God." And from cover to cover, the Bible trumpets the glorious truth that God loves you and is working out a marvelous plan to bring you close to Himself forever.

How can you respond, except to love Him in return? You love Him because He first loved you. Your love is responsive. God is the initiator; you are the responder. And that is why the New Testament writers are always seeking to draw your attention to the love of God, manifested most clearly in His sending His Son to die for you.

Through faith in the crucified and risen Jesus, you get vitally connected to God and His amazing love. As you dwell in Him, you dwell in love, and His love is perfected in you. And what is the result of your love being perfected? You have boldness in the day of judgment and your experience of His complete love casts out all fear.

You have no fear of the consequences of your wicked past, because that has been fully erased by God. He has declared you justified.

You have no fear of the present, because God is watching over you and nothing can happen to you but what He allows to happen. And if God allows it to happen, then it's for a good reason and purpose. Certain of God's complete love for you, now you can face the issues of life without fear.

You have no fear of the future, because you remain in His love. Whatever comes, the Lord will be with you. He's going to keep you and sustain you and you have no cause to be afraid. Perfect love casts out all fear.

You have no fear of the eternal future or of standing before God at the judgment, for Jesus has promised that He is preparing a place for you. And if He prepares a place for you, He promised He would come again and take you to Himself, that where He is, there you might be also. You know the end of the story. Although that story may take some unexpected turns and twists, and though you may have a lot of questions and mysteries along the way, and though you may not be able to understand all that's happening, and though you may wonder what possible good can come out of some difficult episode—still you know the end of the story: they lived happily ever after. And so you have no fear of the eternal future, because you know you're going to be with Him, world without end.

Oh, may your heart draw close to Him this day. May you dwell in Him, abide in His love, and may His love be perfected in your life.

And yet there is more!

Learn for Eternity

The apostle John makes an amazing statement at the very end of his gospel. As he looks back over the book he has written, and even further back over his few glorious years with the Savior, he writes,

> And there are also many other things that Jesus did, which if they were written one by one, I suppose that even the world itself could not contain the books that would be written. Amen (John 21:25).

John therefore reports that Jesus did and said many things that didn't get recorded. John selected a few of them so that his readers would believe that Jesus is the Messiah. A host of sayings and incidents could have been written that were not written. Just enough got recorded so that you could know that Jesus is the Son of God, and that by believing in Him you can have eternal life.

So then, is the rest of the story lost? Not a chance.

Throughout all of eternity, the rest of the story can be told. Throughout the ages to come, God shall reveal to you the boundless treasures of His love toward you. It's going to take all of eternity for you to know it all! You have been given just enough in the Bible to get you into His presence forever—and once you're there, you'll have plenty of time to learn the rest. For centuries without end, God shall reveal the exceeding richness of His love and kindness toward you in Christ Jesus! You and I simply have to thank Him for that.

Father, we thank You for Your amazing love. We praise You for showing us how deeply You love us. Help us to rest in that love. Give us the strength and wisdom to receive Your love, to respond with loving hearts to that love, and to share Your love with others. Fill us, Father, with Your Spirit of love, and enable us to accurately reflect to the world Your burning heart of love. In Jesus' precious name we pray, amen.